TACKLING THE
COLLEGE PAPER

STUDENTS HELPING STUDENTS

TACKLING THE COLLEGE PAPER

A PRENTICE HALL
PRESS BOOK

THE BERKLEY PUBLISHING GROUP
Published by the Penguin Group
Penguin Group (USA) Inc.
375 Hudson Street, New York, New York 10014, USA
Penguin Group (Canada), 10 Alcorn Avenue, Toronto, Ontario M4V 3B2, Canada
(a division of Pearson Penguin Canada Inc.)
Penguin Books Ltd., 80 Strand, London WC2R 0RL, England
Penguin Group Ireland, 25 St. Stephen's Green, Dublin 2, Ireland
(a division of Penguin Books Ltd)
Penguin Group (Australia), 250 Camberwell Road, Camberwell, Victoria 3124, Australia
(a division of Pearson Australia Group Pty. Ltd.)
Penguin Books India Pvt. Ltd., 11 Community Centre, Panchsheel Park, New Delhi—110 017, India
Penguin Group (NZ), cnr. Airborne and Rosedale Roads, Albany, Auckland 1310, New Zealand
(a division of Pearson New Zealand Ltd.)
Penguin Books (South Africa) (Pty.) Ltd., 24 Sturdee Avenue, Rosebank, Johannesburg 2196, South Africa
Penguin Books Ltd., Registered Offices: 80 Strand, London WC2R 0RL, England

Copyright © 2005 by Natavi Guides, Inc.
Text design by Tiffany Estreicher
Cover design and art by Liz Sheehan

ISBN: 0-7352-0397-0

PRINTING HISTORY
Prentice Hall Press trade paperback edition / August 2005

The Prentice Hall Press logo is a trademark belonging to Penguin Group (USA) Inc.

This book has been cataloged by the Library of Congress

PRINTED IN THE UNITED STATES OF AMERICA

10 9 8 7 6 5 4 3 2 1

No doubt you've been bombared with "expert" advice from your parents, professors, and countless advisors. It's time you got advice you can really use—from fellow students who've been where you're headed.

All Students Helping Students® books are written and edited by top students and recent grads from colleges and universities across the United States. You'll find no preachy or condescending advice here—just stuff to help you succeed in tackling your academic, social, and professional challenges.

To learn more about Students Helping Students® books, read samples and student-written articles, share your own experiences with other students, suggest a topic, or ask questions, visit us at www.StudentsHelpingStudents.com!

We're always looking for fresh minds and new ideas!

A Note from the Founders of Students Helping Students®:

Dear Reader,

Welcome to Students Helping Students®!

Before you dive headfirst into reading this book, we wanted to take a moment to share with you where Students Helping Students® came from and where we're headed.

It was only a few years ago that we graduated from college, having made enough mistakes to fill a *War and Peace*-sized novel, learned more and different things than we expected going in, and made some tough decisions—often without having enough advice to help us out. As we thought about our college experiences, we realized that some of the best and most practical advice we ever got came from our classmates and recent grads. And that's how the idea for Students Helping Students® books was born.

Our vision for Students Helping Students® is simple: Allow high school and college students to learn from fellow students who can share brutally honest and practical advice based on their own experiences. We've designed our books to be brief and to the point—we've been there and know that students don't have a minute to waste. They are extremely practical, easy to read, and inexpensive, so they don't empty your wallet.

As with all firsts, we're bound to do some things wrong, and if you have reactions or ideas to share with us, we can't wait to hear them. Visit www.StudentsHelpingStudents.com to submit your comments online.

Thanks for giving us a shot!

—Nataly and Avi
Creators of Students Helping Students®

Student Editors

Scott Grinsell is a junior at Williams College, where he plans to major in history. At Williams, Scott is a representative on the College Council, a Junior Advisor, and the coordinator of a tutoring program for at-risk high school students. As a freshman, he was nominated by one of his professors to be a tutor in the Writing Workshop.

Scott has won numerous awards for his writing, but they're all from his mom.

Nataly Kogan graduated from Wesleyan University in 1998. Her high-honors thesis was entitled "Rule Evasion in Post-Soviet Russia." Nataly, together with her advisor, published articles based on her thesis in several academic journals and as a chapter in an anthology from Oxford University Press.

Student Contributors

Students from Amherst College, Brown University, Bryn Mawr College, Carleton College, Columbia University, Cornell University, Fairleigh Dickinson University, Franklin and Marshall

College, Hampshire College, Harvard University, Haverford College, Middlebury College, New York University, Northwestern University, Princeton University, Santa Clara University, the University of Chicago, the University of Oregon, the University of Pennsylvania, the University of Wisconsin–Madison, Wesleyan University, Williams College, and Vassar College contributed to this guide.

Scott's Note

Even though most of us wrote papers in high school, writing the first few papers in college can be very intimidating. Writing might not have been your best friend in high school. You might not be sure about what your professor expects from you. The topic might seem too broad. Or maybe you're just overwhelmed with college in general.

Try to relax. A college paper is a chance to be creative and say something interesting about the material in class. You don't need to write something worthy of publication in a journal or a book. And since you'll probably write more than a few papers in college, you have a chance to improve your writing with each one.

I hope this guide gives you a feeling of confidence as you start writing. We've tried to break down the process of writing a paper into digestible bites and to point out a few tips to make your task easier. By the time you finish reading you'll be able to plan and write a great paper without losing sleep—or at least not all of it!

Nataly's Note

When I was writing the chapter on writing your senior thesis, my own thesis experience was still fresh in my mind. And the first thing I remembered is that it was everything but easy. A senior thesis is not just a longer version of a regular college paper: It's much more complex in scope and argument and it requires you to work so much harder to create a great final product. But for me it was also a more enjoyable project than many of my college papers because it was truly my own creation: I got to choose the topic, my sources, my arguments, and how and when I wrote the actual thesis.

I hope that however intimidating, working on your senior thesis will be a rewarding experience for you and one that makes you glow with pride when you look at your bound thesis lying on the coffee table. (I can guarantee you that your parents will definitely glow with pride!) It's a huge task, but you have your whole college education to draw upon to help you tackle it. And hopefully the few suggestions we've included in this guide will come in handy as well.

Table of Contents

What It Is

A college paper is a short piece of writing that makes a claim and sustains an argument supporting it. A typical paper assignment in the humanities can range anywhere from a one-page response to thirty pages of original research. The first few papers you write in college will probably be between one and ten pages.

It's unlikely that your first paper will involve much research. In most first-year courses, professors will probably ask you to write about materials you've covered in class. In this guide, we've assumed that you're writing a paper based on course materials, but we've also included a section that gives some advice about approaching papers based on independent research.

However long the assignment is, your paper must have a main point—the infamous thesis. Your high school English teachers probably insisted that your papers have theses, and you're probably used to writing short papers that make a central claim. A thesis gives a paper focus and makes it a piece of academic writing.

A paper also needs evidence supporting the thesis. You might have been able to trick a few high school teachers by skillfully repeating your thesis in different ways for two or three pages. College professors won't be fooled as easily. They want to know why your thesis is valid and you should show this by using supporting arguments and evidence.

Your college papers will allow you to be much more flexible and creative than your high school assignments, and while writing your first few papers can be intimidating, you'll have much more control over how and what you write in them. Have some fun with your papers. It might be tough to believe but it's possible to actually enjoy writing, especially when you get to choose your own topics.

What It's Not

A college paper is not a five-paragraph essay. Many of the papers you wrote in high school might have fit this standard format: a one-paragraph introduction, plus three supporting paragraphs, plus a conclusion. College papers tend to be more complex in their structure and vary significantly by discipline. You'll have to be more flexible and more creative in your approach.

At the same time, a college paper is not a doctoral dissertation. You don't need to forge new academic territory or say anything terribly profound. You do need to make a strong case supporting and analyzing a particular thesis, and do it through clear and error-free writing.

You'll probably write dozens of papers in college. Each time you sit down to write, you'll have better intuition about how to organize your paper and a better feeling for language and style. Your writing will improve organically as you read more, interact with your professors, and hear their comments on your writing. So if you have a hard time with your first few papers, don't throw in the towel. No one expects you to know how to write well from the start and you can improve your writing skills over time.

1

Getting Started

It's useful to think of your paper as the culmination of your experience in a particular class. All of your reading, all of your time in class, and all of the hours you spend thinking about the course materials will be part of your paper—either directly or by providing you with relevant background. If you learn a ton about a certain subject—whether it's early American poetry or the sociology of Japanese cell phone use—you'll be able to draw on that material when you write your paper.

To that end, absorbing as much as you can from your classes will actually help you write better papers—and get better grades. Don't skip too many lectures, take notes, pay attention to your professor's preferences, and try to do at least some of each week's reading. That way, when the time comes to write a paper, you'll be in great shape.

- (Almost) Perfect Attendance
- Write It Down
- Read Along
- Know What Your Professors Want
- Plan Ahead

(Almost) Perfect Attendance

Not every college class is interesting, many are scheduled way too early in the morning, and some are taught by professors who care too little about teaching. All of that—combined with the fact that you're pretty overwhelmed with academics, extracurriculars, your roommate's music blasting, and oh, that tempting sound of fun down the hall—can serve as a great excuse to skip class.

Try not to give into the temptation too often. You'll be wasting your tuition money and your college time, but more practically, you'll be missing out on a lot of learning that can help you ace your papers and exams.

If your class has a discussion component, try to participate as much as possible. When something comes to mind and it seems appropriate, don't hesitate to raise your hand and say it. Some of the best paper topics come out of these kinds of informal exchanges in class, where one student proposes an interpretation and the professor and other students comment on it.

Even if you don't have an opportunity to participate out loud, try to really think about the material during class. If you're stuck at the back of a dark lecture hall, it might be tempting to just sit back and write down what the professor says. Instead, try to think of ways that you might challenge your professor's ideas, and write down questions that come to mind. Your question might later lead to a paper topic or might make you think of something else that does.

Write It Down

You might have been able to get through high school without taking notes. You may not think of yourself as the note-taking type. You may not even own a notebook.

Get one. Taking notes can make writing papers much easier because you'll have a summary of what was covered in class and what core issues you might want to discuss in your paper. Many professors use class time to emphasize what parts of the material they consider the most important for you to learn. Write those down. You'll want to make sure to touch on these points when you write your paper.

There are so many ways to take notes and you probably have one that works for you already. Some people meticulously outline each major point covered in class; others find it quite sufficient to write down a few brief words or phrases. Do what works for you and don't worry about what you should be doing. The key is to write down just enough to jar your memory later on when you look over your notes.

What you shouldn't do is try to write down every word that comes out of your professor's mouth. None of us can write and listen well at the same time and you don't want to miss what's going on in class because you're too busy highlighting in your notebook. Write down the main ideas and make sure that you write legibly enough to make sense of your notes later. Use stars, arrows, circles, funny faces, and exclamation points—whatever works for you—to emphasize particularly important details.

Read Along

More than anything else, doing your reading is essential to writing a good paper. Not just doing the reading, but doing it critically and extracting the main ideas from it. This will really help you when you're trying to think of a good topic or thesis.

—Sophomore
Cornell University

When you're in a class based primarily on papers, the more you read, the more options you'll have for paper topics. Say, for example, you're taking a class on medieval Bavarian literature. The more you've read about medieval Bavaria, the better intuition you'll have about the topic, and the more things you'll have to say about it. Even if you don't write a paper about every Bavarian poem you read, each one will add to your intuitive grasp of Bavarian literature. So, when you write your paper about the symbolism of beer steins (mugs) in medieval Bavarian epics, you'll be more confident and better informed.

Of course, you don't have to read every paragraph of every book or article that your professor assigns. We've all had a few professors who think it's important to read every page of a book when only two chapters are relevant to the course. Try to skim through the material and judge what parts are most relevant to the core of what you're learning in class. One way to do this is to read the first few paragraphs of each chapter or section.

Another great guide to what and how much you should read is your professor—pay attention to what points he or she emphasize in class and make sure to read up on those.

In general, it's a good idea to do most of the reading at the beginning on each semester. That way, you'll learn what you need to read carefully and what, if anything, you can skim or skip completely.

If you know what the majority of your class reading covers, you'll have much more flexibility when choosing your paper topic and enough background to structure your initial arguments and ideas. This will really help. You want to avoid having to read huge chunks of class material for the first time after your paper is assigned. You won't have enough time to really absorb it all and this can be frustrating.

> Before I even begin to sit down to write my outline I always make sure I've read all the relevant sources, underlined and dog-eared important pages, and generally understood the ideas of the texts.
>
> —Sophomore
> Vassar College

Know What Your Professors Want

Besides the obvious benefits of getting to know some pretty smart people, knowing your professors can help you write better papers and get higher grades. Professors are people with personal tastes. Each one has subjective preferences and quirks. Get to know what these are and don't ignore them in your papers. While a solid, clearly written paper will fare well in most classes, understanding what your particular professor is looking for can also help.

For example, some professors obsess about students sticking extremely close to assigned topics and class material. Others

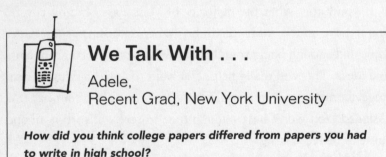

We Talk With . . .

Adele,
Recent Grad, New York University

How did you think college papers differed from papers you had to write in high school?
I figured out at some point during my sophomore year that college professors are not only trying to teach you the facts so that you memorize and regurgitate them, but so that you can take a bunch of facts and start putting them together in a coherent and logical manner. High school papers were all about "the right answer" or writing what the teacher wanted to read, and of course, I sometimes fell into those traps in college, too. But I did realize at some point that, above all, the professors are interested in how you think.

What was the most difficult paper you wrote in college? Why was it so difficult?
The most difficult papers that I wrote in college were the ones that I really didn't want to write. Either the class was boring or the subject just wasn't my bag. I would procrastinate until the night before, when I ended up pulling an all-nighter. The material for those kinds of papers never got more interesting at 3:00 am, but the adrenaline was probably what got me through them.

What was most helpful to you in getting your college papers done?
For the papers that I really wanted to write, talking to the professor and to other students who were interested in the same subject really helped. I would go in to talk to the professor after I had written a loose draft and had some ideas that needed fleshing out. Discussion was really key in those situations. The papers that I really didn't want to write were another story—probably it was the fear of getting an incomplete that helped me finish them. I knew that the chances of actually writing the paper would get slimmer and slimmer as time passed after the deadline.

What advice would you give to college students about writing college papers?
I would advise that you read and write carefully. For any paper that you have to write, you need to do a lot of reading first. Take a lot of notes in the margins—that's what's going to get your paper started: the little sparks of inspiration that you get while reading. Then, of course, you have to write very carefully—professors are a lot tougher on you when they see sloppy mistakes like spelling and grammar errors, no matter how great your ideas are.

want you to extrapolate from specific topics to broader issues. The better you know your professor's preferences—read "requirements"—the more you'll know about shaping your paper.

Go to your professor's office hours. Talk about the class, the paper topic, what questions you have, and what ideas you might like to explore in your paper. Ask your professor about his or her interests—listening to how your professor talks about books, articles, or even other papers can reveal quite a bit about what he or she might expect from you in class. And don't worry about imposing—most professors appreciate when students show interest in their class and will be happy to talk to you. Besides, it's their job.

Plan Ahead

It's a pretty good idea to start working on your paper as soon as possible, especially if you're a bit anxious about it. You don't need to churn out ten drafts before the paper is due, but you should keep the due date in mind when you receive your class syllabus.

In many courses, you may not be able to start your paper very far in advance, mostly because you won't have done the reading necessary to answer your professor's question. Usually, your professor will give you paper topics about a week or two in advance of when the paper is due. When you get the assignment, make a plan for how you'll tackle it—and keep in mind what other deadlines you have for other classes.

You might find it helpful to put together a brief timeline. Set a few rough dates for figuring out your topic and thesis, sketching your outline, writing your first draft, and finishing your revisions.

As you'll probably find, however, writing doesn't always happen on a schedule. You may encounter problems in your first draft that you hadn't initially expected, or you may have a harder time resisting the lure of throwing around a frisbee on the sunny quad lawn. If you make a timeline, give yourself some flexibility. Instead of holding yourself rigidly to the dates that you initially set, use them as indicators. If a certain step of the process takes you a bit longer than you planned, you'll be able to judge how much time you have left to get the rest done.

I would advise college students to not leave the thinking through of the paper to the last minute. Talk a lot in class when the professor assigns the paper to exchange ideas in the classroom setting and make sure you have a clear understanding of the assignment. Then, scratch out a draft, no matter how rough and unclear, and bring it to the professor to discuss and dissect. One on one, professors are usually much more willing to talk to you about what they want the paper to cover, how they want you to attack the topic, and how you can mold your ideas into a powerful piece of writing.

—Recent Grad
New York University

2

Developing a Topic and a Thesis

In high school, choosing a paper topic probably wasn't something you thought about too much. If you read *Moby Dick* in your English class, then you might have had to write a paper on it in response to a specific question from your teacher. In college, courses tend to move much faster and cover a much wider range of material. As a result, you'll often have the ability to choose what you write about.

Once you find a topic, the challenge is finding something to argue about it. Carefully think about what your paper will say at the beginning of the process and it will help you write more clearly as you develop your argument and analysis. All good papers begin with an original and interesting idea that becomes the paper's thesis—the main point that you'll present to the reader.

- Clarity Counts
- Don't Choose in Isolation
- I'm Interested in . . .
- Topic First, Thesis Second
- If You're Stuck, Freewrite and Brainstorm
- Do a Thesis Doubletake
- Don't Get Too Attached to Your Thesis

Clarity Counts

Assuming that you have a choice about your topic, you'll probably either be asked to select one from a list of assigned topics or questions, or be given free reign to come up with one of your own. For first-year seminars and introductory-level classes, it's pretty common to receive a list of possible topics to which you can add with permission from the professor.

Take a few minutes to read through the list of topics your professor hands out and see what comes to mind. Jot down a few ideas about each one, and think about which interests you the most. It helps to look through some of your class notes or materials to jar your memory—especially if some of the topics deal with material you covered a few weeks back. There's no need to reread everything you might use. Just skim through what you think is important.

Your paper topic should be very clear and you should know exactly what you're writing about. Try this: See if you can summarize your topic in a single sentence. If not, rethink it and see if you need to reduce the scope or choose a better-organized central theme.

Your topic should also be pretty specific. Unless you're asked to synthesize or summarize all of the material you've covered—ouch!—you shouldn't try to write a paper about everything you've learned in class. Pick one idea, one historical period, one book, one theme, two things or concepts to compare, or a particular theory—but do pick and don't drive yourself crazy by trying to include everything.

Choosing your own topic can sometimes be a lot more difficult than choosing from a list of assigned topics. You have a blank canvas in front of you and you have to figure out how to fill it. Don't panic. A good way to think of topics is to go through some of the class material you found particularly interesting and ask questions about it.

Take our Bavarian literature class as an example. A few questions you could consider are:

✓ What are some prevalent themes in Bavarian poetry?
✓ What are some similarities between Bavarian poetry and the poetry of other countries?
✓ How are historical events reflected in Bavarian literature?

Your answers to broad questions like these can become valid topics. For example, you might end up writing about the symbolism of beer steins in Bavarian poetry.

When thinking about your topic, consider the number of pages that you have to fill. If you're writing a three-page paper, maybe you shouldn't write a comparison of five artistic movements or ideas. Try starting with two.

Some people like to choose the topic they think is the "hardest," but that's silly. There isn't a clearly defined set of criteria that identify certain topics as the hardest, and most professors try to make paper topics similar in scope and depth. By trying to choose the most difficult topic, you risk missing out on writing about something that genuinely interests you and has a much greater chance of producing a great paper.

Don't worry if you can't choose a topic right away. Sometimes the best ideas for papers will come at breakfast between bites of a Pop-Tart. Give your thoughts some time to percolate. But keep in mind that you'll only be able to do this if you've planned ahead and left yourself a good chunk of time to think about your paper.

 Scott's Corner

In my English class last spring, we received a list of possible topics for our first paper on Victorian poetry. I picked the topic that I thought had the most depth and that seemed the most challenging to me.

As I sat down with my professor during office hours to explain my approach to the question, I got a blank stare. I realized immediately that I had missed the point of her question.

On her advice, I abandoned the topic for a new one. In place of a topic that seemed outwardly hard, I chose one that I really cared about. The paper turned out to be one of the best I've written in college so far.

Don't Choose in Isolation

You don't have to figure out your paper topic all on your own. Talk to your class TA and spend a few minutes discussing your topic with your professor. You'll find that these discussions are most useful when you already have a few ideas about your topic and are looking for more specific feedback than the answer to the question: "What do you think I should write about?"

Try to take your professor's suggestions to heart, especially if he or she thinks that your topic is too broad in scope. Professors have seen more than a few students try to take on a topic for a five-page paper that is more suitable for a book. Get some advice and you'll save yourself unnecessary frustration later on.

I'm Interested in . . .

As you think about possible books, authors, or issues to write about, try to pick something you find interesting. If you don't care at all about your topic, the hours you spend at the keyboard or in the library will be unnecessarily painful. And you're much more likely to write a great paper and do well if you're writing about something that you find at least moderately interesting.

The wonderful thing about college is that you can usually choose what you write about, even if you have to choose from a list. Take advantage of that. Each topic can be approached in a dozen different ways and you should be able to find a way that interests you the most.

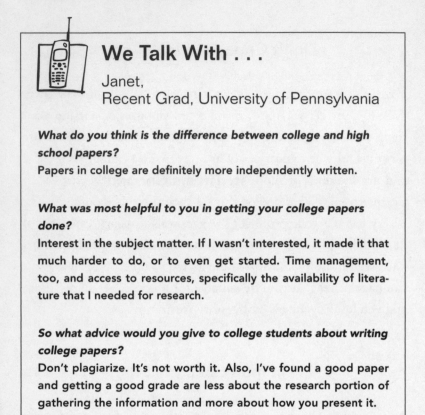

We Talk With . . .

Janet,
Recent Grad, University of Pennsylvania

What do you think is the difference between college and high school papers?
Papers in college are definitely more independently written.

What was most helpful to you in getting your college papers done?
Interest in the subject matter. If I wasn't interested, it made it that much harder to do, or to even get started. Time management, too, and access to resources, specifically the availability of literature that I needed for research.

So what advice would you give to college students about writing college papers?
Don't plagiarize. It's not worth it. Also, I've found a good paper and getting a good grade are less about the research portion of gathering the information and more about how you present it.

Think about it this way: You have to write the paper anyway, so why not be interested in what you're writing about?

You'll always write better when you're interested in what you're writing, interested in learning about the topic, and interested in explaining it to others. Try to find a topic that really brings into focus the crux of the subject matter or the course. Writing about myths about George Washington's false teeth may sound more interesting to research, but you'll get more out of that American history class—and you'll find more relevant material—if you write about his relationship with the other founders.

—Sophomore
Northwestern University

Topic First, Thesis Second

Once you've picked a general topic for your paper, you need to come up with a thesis. Your thesis is the main and focal point of your paper and it's the position you'll take on your particular topic. A paper is not a paper without a strong thesis, so spend some extra time thinking about it.

A good way to move from a topic to a thesis is to try to rephrase your topic as a question. For example, if you're writing about beer steins in a Bavarian poem, you might ask: "What is the meaning of the beer steins in this Bavarian poem?"

Your answer to the question may very well be an argument you make in your paper, or your thesis: "The beer steins serve as a symbol for masculine insecurity."

A thesis is a claim that you can argue for or against. It should be something that you can present persuasively and clearly in the scope of your paper, so keep in mind the page count. If possible, your thesis should also be somewhat original.

Your thesis should make an analytical argument. That is, it should go beyond summary. To make sure this is the case, you should ask yourself whether someone could contend that your thesis is wrong. If so, you have succeeded in proposing an analytical argument.

—Junior
Columbia University

To give you a better idea of what not to do, here are some examples of not-so-great theses:

- Germany lost World War II.
- *Crime and Punishment* is about death.
- Is the Cold War really over?

One is a fact, one is a half-baked interpretation, and one is a question. All of them have an element that sounds vaguely thesis-like, but they all fall short of being real theses. The first statement isn't really controversial and you can't make a great argument about it. The second is too vague and needs a bit more focus. The third statement doesn't make a claim, but asks a question. It's a first step to a thesis, but it's not one yet.

All of these statements have the kernel of an idea. To turn them into theses, it's important to add a touch of justification and explanation. For example, "Germany lost World War II because Hitler's expansionist vision spiraled out of control toward the end of the war." This could be a thesis. It makes a point that can be argued for and against, and it's one that can be reasonably supported with evidence.

If You're Stuck, Freewrite
and Brainstorm

We all get stuck from time to time. If you can't think of a thesis, it sometimes helps to turn on your computer—or open up a notebook—and start writing about a topic until you have something resembling an argument. Burn some incense, slip on your Birkenstock sandals, and let the intellectual juices flow. Don't worry about style or structure. Just try to get some ideas down on paper.

See where this process takes you. Usually, after a page or two, you'll have a clearer idea of what you want to write about. Press print, and scan through the pages to see where you might have come to a thesis. When you find it, circle it. Rephrase it, if necessary, to make it sound clearer and more specific. (Refer to the previous section for some general thesis guidelines.)

Another way to develop a thesis without actually writing full pages of text is to pull out some scratch paper and start scribbling down whatever words and concepts come to mind about your topic. Don't worry about them making sense initially. Get a few concepts and ideas down on paper and then read over them to see if any can evolve into a thesis.

Freewriting and brainstorming are great ways to get you thinking and get your mind out of a temporary warp. Give them a shot and try not to worry about spending this extra time: If you don't have a strong thesis, your paper will suffer and you'll have a hard time writing it.

Do a Thesis Doubletake

Try not to write for the grade. Ask yourself, can people read this paper and feel like they learned something? Try to say something that isn't obvious.

—Junior
Haverford College

Once you have a rough idea for your thesis, take a few minutes and test it out. That way, you won't write three pages and realize that it's flawed or misguided. Here are a few ways to make sure that your thesis will help lead to a strong argument and a well-structured paper:

- ✓ Read your thesis out loud. Does it make sense to you? Does it make clear what your main point is? Remember, you can argue for or against your thesis, but the reader of your paper should be able to know your position as soon as he or she reads your thesis statement.
- ✓ Show your thesis statement to a few of your friends who aren't taking your class and ask them if it makes sense. Do they understand what it means, or do they look like Bambi caught in the headlights of an eighteen-wheeler? Your thesis should make sense even to someone who knows nothing about your class, so consider your friends' reactions carefully.
- ✓ Does your thesis answer all parts of your professor's question? If you have an assigned topic, it's critical that you

tackle the entire issue in the way that you're asked to. If the question asks you to "explain the most important causes and effects of the fall of the Soviet Union," your thesis needs to address both the causes and the effects.

✓ Check the scope of your thesis. Are you trying to argue something that can be argued in the required length of your paper or are you taking on the history of the world in five pages?

✓ Is your thesis controversial just for the sake of being controversial? It's fantastic if you have an original idea, but make sure that your thesis isn't simply absurd. In high school, some of your teachers might have given you a good grade for taking a contrary position, just because it had some element of originality. College professors probably won't be that generous. Most of them have spent more years than you have been alive thinking about their subjects, and they can tell the difference between a thesis that is trying to be "out there" and one that is genuinely original. Having a unique thesis is great, but you still have to make sure that you can reasonably argue it in your paper.

Try very hard to make your thesis as direct, coherent, and well written as possible. Having a clear thesis is not just important for the reader to understand your paper; it's also important to make sure you have a complete understanding of what it is you want to say.

—Sophomore
Vassar College

Don't Get Too Attached to Your Thesis

Regardless of how hard you work to come up with a strong, clear, and original thesis, chances are that it will change somewhat before you're done with your paper. As you get more involved with your topic and the specifics of each part of your arguments, you'll probably come up with some ideas and conclusions that are different from your original thesis.

That happens a lot, so try not to get frustrated. Part of the reason professors make us write papers is to force us to think about the class material in depth. And when we think about something for a long time, we're bound to change our initial position or opinion. As you write your paper, always refer back to your original thesis and see if you still think it's valid. If you need to tweak it a bit, do it. Just because you initially thought it was a great thesis doesn't mean you have to stick to it.

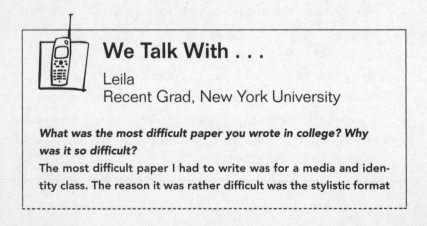

We Talk With . . .
Leila
Recent Grad, New York University

What was the most difficult paper you wrote in college? Why was it so difficult?
The most difficult paper I had to write was for a media and identity class. The reason it was rather difficult was the stylistic format

of the paper. The professor was introducing a new teaching method and our papers had to reflect a particular methodology along with our argument. It was a challenge because I had never written a paper with a particular teaching methodology in mind.

What was most helpful to you in getting your college papers done?
Honestly, the most helpful thing was keeping an open mind about the subject, trying to examine the argument from all angles. The MLA handbook was also a necessity.

What advice would you give to college students about writing college papers?
Don't wait until the last minute before starting a paper.

3

Making a Plan

Now that you have a good thesis, you need to come up with analyses and arguments to support it. You probably already have some idea of where you want to go with your paper, but you might find it helpful to pause and make a brief outline of your main points and arguments. Even if you're rushed for time, take a few minutes to think about the layout and organization of your paper. Knowing where your paper is headed will help you a great deal when you actually begin to write it.

- Get Organized
- Roman Numerals Galore
- Laser-Sharp (Thesis) Focus
- Counterarguments, Beware!
- You're in Charge, Not Your Outline
- It's Office-Hours Time

Get Organized

When you start developing an overall plan for your paper, surround yourself with your books and notes from class. This sounds obvious, but it's easy to write an entire outline for a paper without ever walking across your dorm room to pull a few books off the shelf.

Have access to books that are related to your topic even if you don't plan to specifically use them in your paper. Sometimes as you're writing your outline, you may decide to revise your thesis to include another source. You may find that a thoughtful comparison with another work, even if it's only one sentence long, can illuminate your entire argument.

If you're surrounded by materials from class, you'll also get into the right mindset for thinking about your paper. Simply being immersed in your class notes will get you thinking about the subject as a whole and help you come with up with ideas for your paper.

Roman Numerals Galore

I find it helpful to first take notes on everything I think might be a relevant fact or quote in a book. Then I compile all of my notes from all of my sources and categorize each one. For example, "background," "point A," or "related to B and C." Then I prioritize and order just those category titles—if there are a lot, some may be subsections of another—and then I've got a great start to a coherent outline."

—Sophomore
Northwestern University

Probably none of us got through high school without writing at least a few detailed outlines, especially for research papers. It's not a bad idea to have an outline, but it doesn't have to be long or very formal. Its main goal is to serve as the road map for your paper, to capture the overall structure and flow of your main points and arguments.

Start by writing your thesis at the top of the page—the point of the outline is to find a layout for your paper that most effectively argues your thesis. Look at the phrasing of your thesis and your professor's question. Is there a structure implicit in either one? For example, if you're writing an analysis of *Hamlet,* does it make sense to write about its overall structure before you start writing about the specific language structures? Try to find an organization that develops naturally from your thesis.

Also, think in terms of sections before you start thinking in terms of paragraphs. In high school, your thesis could probably be supported in one section. Each paragraph focused on one piece of supporting evidence that related directly to your thesis. Your theses for papers in college will often have multiple parts. Each section of your paper will probably contain a few paragraphs, which support a part of your thesis. Not all papers will break down into multiple sections, but most of them will work out that way.

Scott's Corner

I tend to use a different outlining method depending on what kind of paper I'm writing, and how comfortable I am with the topic. Sometimes, when I'm writing a compare-and-contrast paper, I find it helpful to sketch a large chart with each item as a column, and each subtopic as a row.

If I'm writing a more freeflowing argument, I sometimes write a very rough prose outline with no formal structure. I'll write a word or two for things I know a lot about, and write more for areas that I still want to think about. I find that this combination of freewriting and outlining is a great way to refine my thesis and develop language to use in my first draft.

As you work on your outline, don't obsess about outlining every paragraph and getting down every detail. You'll drive yourself crazy and spend time writing in your outline what you should be writing in your paper. And if you get too bogged down in details, you'll risk losing track of the overall flow of your paper. Instead, write down your main arguments and ideas in an order that makes them most powerful, and then fill in the details when you actually begin to write.

There's always a question about how to order your main arguments to make them most effective. There's no science to determine this and you should rely on your logic and intuition to figure it out. Keep in mind that people remember what they read first and last better than what they read in the middle, so you

We Talk With . . .

Ryan,
Senior, Santa Clara University

What is the biggest difference between college papers and high school papers, in your opinion?
It really depends on the class and the topic. High school papers follow a basic formula, the five-paragraph essay, and I never wrote anything longer than twelve pages. In college I've definitely written much longer papers and a lot more often. There's also a lot less guidance and feedback along the way with college papers: no peer editing, no getting a rough draft back from a teacher before the final copy. The whole process isn't as structured in college.

What kind of tools/methods do you use to help organize yourself when writing a paper?
I always write outlines. In fact, any decent paper that I've ever written had an outline first.

might want to put your strongest argument either at the beginning or the end of your paper.

Once you have the overall structure of your paper laid out, you can think about what each of the smaller sections might contain. Jot down a few notes for each, indicating to yourself what specific points you'll want to cover.

Check out the simple outline template on the next page. It's not rocket science, but it might help you lay out your thoughts and get organized. Feel free to change it to fit your needs and the specific format of your paper.

Sample Outline Template

Here's a template that you can use to structure your outline. Adapt it to you particular needs and use it to help you focus your research and writing.

Overall topic	
Thesis statement	
Supporting argument #1 • Main evidence (a) • Main evidence (b)	
Supporting argument #2 • Main evidence (a) • Main evidence (b)	
Supporting argument #3 • Main evidence (a) • Main evidence (b)	

Laser-Sharp (Thesis) Focus

Remember that all of this planning and outlining you're doing is for a reason: You want to organize your paper in a way that most effectively presents and argues your thesis statement. After you've got it down, take a look at your brief outline and see if you've accomplished this. Here are some questions to consider:

- ✓ Do your main arguments sound convincing?
- ✓ Do they address your main thesis?
- ✓ Are your arguments presented in the most persuasive order?
- ✓ Can you argue them reasonably well with the information from your class materials?
- ✓ Do you have enough evidence to support each argument?

Counterarguments, Beware!

As you write your outline, consider possible objections to your arguments and your thesis. If someone reading your paper disagreed with your thesis, what would they say? How would they respond to the arguments you're making?

The best and most persuasive papers take on counterarguments in the open rather than ignoring them or just mentioning them in passing. There are very few, if any, arguments in the world that cannot be argued against. Think about counterarguments to your thesis and use them in your paper to make it stronger and more balanced.

You can fit counterarguments into your paper in different ways. You can group them together in one section or you can discuss each of them in the section of your paper where each is most relevant. Think about your topic and your thesis and see which option works best.

But don't just acknowledge that there are points of view that disagree with your arguments. Explore each counterargument in the context of your topic and explain why your thesis is still valid even though this particular counterargument exists. Is the counterargument weak? Invalid? Valid but not relevant to your particular thesis? Find what makes the counterargument weaker than your own argument and explain this in your paper.

You're in Charge, Not Your Outline

If you use your outline too carefully, your paper can become overly choppy. Try to be flexible.

—Sophomore
Cornell University

Try to avoid thinking of your outline as a precise plan for your paper. It's more like an artist's sketch than an architect's blueprint. An outline is supposed to give you a sense of where you're going, but it shouldn't include every step along the way. As you write, you'll probably discover new issues you want to address

Scott's Corner

I try to avoid even looking at my outline all the time as I write most of my papers. Sometimes, I'll even turn it over as I write so that I'm not tempted to copy whole sentences or phrases from it.

If a paper has a complex and formal structure with lots of parts, I use an outline to keep track of all of my arguments and counter-arguments. But even for papers like that, I try to keep my outline as a reference tool rather than something that dictates my paper.

We Talk With . . .

Rebecca,
Recent Grad, University of
Wisconsin–Madison

How did you think college papers differed from papers you had to write in high school?
In high school, papers were written to show what you know. In college, papers are written to show what you know, what your opinion is about it, how you acquired this knowledge, and how it compares to other things you know.

What was the most difficult paper you wrote in college? Why was it so difficult?
I wrote a very difficult paper about my student teaching experiences. It was very difficult because it summed up two years of full-time teaching into a five-page paper (couldn't be more than that). It's impossible to sum up two years of experiences in five

pages. I felt, handing in the paper, that is was all fluff and had no depth. It didn't really say anything I wanted it to say.

What was most helpful to you in getting your college papers done?
Outlines and lists. It's important to plot out your paper on a graph and it's important to set dates and times to work on your paper, and don't forget time for revisions!

What advice would you give to college students about writing college papers?

1. Gather your information and learn the topic.
2. Outline.
3. Set dates for writing. Stick to them!
4. Proofread and revise.
5. Have others proofread and revise.
6. Revise, yet again.
7. Turn it in on time. There's no excuse if you've set a timeline for yourself.
8. And whatever you do: Do *not* start writing a paper the night before it's due!

and decide that there are some things you can leave out. When you revise your paper, you may end up deleting entire paragraphs or whole sections. Allow yourself the flexibility to do this and avoid being stifled by your own outline.

Some students actually choose not to write outlines at all because they don't want to feel confined by a predefined plan. (Or maybe because they just don't want to bother.) You might be one of those people, and if you feel that you can handle your paper without an outline, you should trust your instincts. Our only suggestion is that you try it once, that you don't make it too detailed and overbearing, and that you see if it makes your life easier. It might.

It's Office-Hours Time

If you're lucky enough to go to a school where you have access to your professors and TAs, you shouldn't feel hesitant about approaching them to talk about your paper. It's helpful to meet with your professor or TA at any stage of the writing process, but it's usually best to do it after you finish your outline. That way you can hear your professor's comments on your thesis and your arguments, without having already committed your ideas to paper.

Some professors and TAs are unwilling to read preliminary drafts, but they'll almost certainly listen to an informal summary of your arguments. Most of them actually enjoy this kind of interaction with students and will be thrilled to talk to you, so give it a try.

> Always meet with your professor. It really helps to discuss your ideas with someone else. They almost always want to help, and it's always a good idea.
>
> —Sophomore
> Carleton College

We Talk With . . .

Jayme,
Sophomore, New York University–Tisch

What is most helpful to you in getting your college papers done?
Sitting down and writing as soon as you get the time. If you can take the time to write before the night before it's due, you'll have time to look over it again. College students are really nice about reading other students papers (even if they're not in the same class) and helping you. Most freshman-year papers are about being able to explain what you've learned to someone who doesn't understand the material or is unaware of what you're learning. Friends, roommates, and hallmates are great people to have read your papers. If they understand what you're trying to say, you've succeeded. If they're clueless then your paper probably needs some reworking.

What advice would you give to college students about writing college papers?
Do the best you can and find out what works for you. Some people need to write in the library, some need to write a few hours before they're due, etc. Everyone is different and you have to find your style. If you're not getting the grades you want, talk to your TA and ask how you can improve (that's what they're there for). Keep in mind that writing papers is subjective. You will have to change the way you write for different professors and TAs. It's best to talk to them before you hand in your papers and understand exactly what they're looking for.

What advice would you give to college students about writing papers the night before?

All-nighters are great and work well for some, but drink lots of coffee, and make sure you have a working printer before you're finished. I know too many people who stayed up all night and then found out their printer was broken and they needed to be in class. Don't do all the work unless you can show it off.

4

Writing Your Paper

If you have a strong thesis and a rough plan for how to lay out the main parts of your paper, actually writing it might turn out to be easier than you think. Keep track of your timeline, take breaks, and don't worry too much about style as you begin to write. You'll have a chance to revise and edit later—unless you're writing your paper the night before it's due.

Keep in mind that writing will probably lead to new ideas, or at least to altering your original thoughts. When we write we become involved with the material and can see issues in a different way from when we're just thinking about them. Don't be afraid to change an argument or supporting details as you write if you think doing so will improve your paper. It's extra work, but it's worth it.

- Don't Rush it
- Write For an Audience

- Think Like a True Academic
- Write Your Introduction Twice
- And Therefore . . .
- Quote Like a Pro
- Stealing Is Wrong
- Style Guide
- All Good Things Must Come to an End
- Work Hard, Play Hard

Don't Rush it

Obviously, you can't always write your papers as far in advance as you'd like. You're running around trying to juggle academics, extracurriculars, parties, friends, sleep, and whatever else you might have piled up on your plate. You absolutely don't have to finish your entire first draft two weeks before the paper is due. But if you start writing with some time ahead of you, you'll feel more in control and less anxious about getting it done on time.

As much as you try to plan your time, you'll probably end up writing most of your paper in the last few days before it's due. That's fine, but if at all possible, leave yourself more than one day to get it done.

Writing ahead of time also removes the sense of urgency—and sometimes, panic—that can make you want to reach the page limit as quickly as possible. You should feel like you have plenty of time to think about what you want to say.

So, sit back, put on a good CD, and plunge into it.

Generally, I'll spend the first day going over my reference materials and formulating my thesis. Then the next two or three days I'll spend on the outline and quotes alone, before I begin writing even a single word of my first draft. Then the remaining three or four days I'll spend on my first and final drafts.

—Junior
Vassar College

MY FIRST COLLEGE ESSAY
by Sadia, Sophomore, New York University

My first college essay was quite an experience. I registered late for the class and was a bit slow in terms of understanding how to use a syllabus. Anyway, during the Tuesday session of my Middle Eastern studies class I learned that my short three-to-five-page paper would be due the next session—that Thursday. From my peers I gathered that there was a particular book I was supposed to use in order to write the paper and, of course, the book was nowhere to be found because all the smart kids had checked the book out of the library. I cursed silently and thought that I would simply not write the paper. But that Wednesday, I tried the New York Public Library and found the book, strangely, on the shelf next to where the call number dictated it would be. I felt destined to write the paper. I arrived at my apartment by 8:00 pm, and finally started the paper by midnight. I began to read. By 2:00 am, I had a paragraph summarizing my research and a vague introduction. By 2:30, I slid under my sheets, my eyelids melting comfortably when I gently closed them. I'll finish the paper tomorrow, I reasoned.

By 6:00 am, I jumped out of bed and begin typing furiously. My eyes squinted from behind my glasses, which were placed somewhat lopsided on my nose. My eyes took time to adjust, but my fingers were constructing sentences on their own. By 9:00 am, I realized that I had decided I wouldn't be attending chemistry because of the paper. I typed about five pages and by 10:00 am, I began editing. My class didn't begin until 2:00, so I figured the shower could be postponed until after class. When I felt my paper had gained some substance, I took a fifteen-minute tea break. And then I sat down to edit. After the tea, I restructured my intro and came up with tangential evidence for my little thesis (linking minstrel shows to 19th-century orientalist paintings). I summarized my thoughts in big enough words and printed out my minimum-three-page handiwork by 1:40. I threw on some dirty jeans and a sweatshirt and ran out of my apartment for class. I had successfully crafted my first college essay—an A paper.

What's most helpful in writing college essays is tricking yourself into thinking they're due before you think they are. That generally doesn't work if you have a sharp memory, but if the assignment due date is far enough away, sometimes it works. If you have time to edit, those B+/A- papers can become A papers.

Write for an Audience

As you write your paper, imagine an audience—a person who is going to read it and who needs to understand what you're writing about. This will help you write more clearly and in a way that best communicates your ideas. Sometimes we are very formal and use tons of big words in our papers so that we sound more academic. Big words are fine, but remember that your main goal is to produce an intelligent and clear paper.

Think of writing as just a bit more polished and formal than talking. There should be no "hmmms" or "ahas" in your paper, and you should not use contractions like "we're" or "I'm" unless it's an extremely informal paper. But there's no need to write long-winded sentences or show off your SAT vocabulary just for the sake of impressing the reader.

Don't hesitate to use a word like "lugubrious" if it seems right to you and fits into the context of your paper, but don't do it just because you think that you'll be the only one in your class to use it. Be smart, but don't go out of your way to sound like you are.

Most professors care about the content and clarity of your

Scott's Corner

When I started writing papers in college, I assumed that I needed to write in a more sophisticated way. At the time, I thought this meant using lots of big words and long sentences. I thought it made my ideas sound more important if I wrote them in a heavily worked, difficult style.

There are two problems with this. One is that I sounded like an arrogant, bratty freshman. The other is that I sometimes got bogged down in my convoluted sentences and lost track of my thesis, or worse, ended up arguing something different than I intended.

I don't shy away from big words and long sentences if I think they're absolutely necessary. On the other hand, I try not to write them for cosmetic appeal. They aren't as pretty as I used to think, anyway.

paper much more than the number of four-syllable words that you use. They want to see that you've grasped the class material and that you can intelligently talk about it in a paper. But some professors have idiosyncrasies that you should know about and you should keep them in mind as you write.

My philosophy professor required that all of us use ten new words in each of our weekly papers. "New" meant that we had to go to the dictionary and find words we'd never heard of before and put them in our papers. It seemed ridiculous and it was, but to get a decent grade we had to do it.

—Senior
Wesleyan University

Think Like a True Academic

In high school, we learned to write one kind of analytical paper that carried us through pretty much any class. In college, you have to learn that each discipline has its own standards for writing.

—Sophomore
Columbia University

Every academic discipline tends to have its own conventions for written work. As you read the books and articles you're assigned over the semester, try to figure out what these conventions are and follow them as much as you can in your papers.

In art history, for example, there is a stronger emphasis on visual description than in most other fields. Sometimes a discipline has special stylistic conventions. For example, in philosophy, it's not unusual to read a paper that begins, "In this paper, I will argue that . . ." In an English class, this kind of opening would probably be frowned upon.

You should find out if your professor expects you to follow any particular style or format in your paper. Professors in intro classes are usually much more flexible and don't expect you to have mastered every nuance of their academic discipline just yet. If your professor does require a certain format, make an effort to follow it.

At the same time, don't get too carried away with the idea that your paper needs to be written for a particular discipline. No matter what subject your paper is about, you'll still be expected to have a thesis, make clear arguments, and present your ideas in an effective and well-written way.

Write Your Introduction Twice

We've all been there: sitting in front of a computer screen, the clock counting down precious minutes, and the cursor blinking impatiently at the top of a blank page. Beginning to write your paper can be tough, kind of like starting to run after standing still for a while—it's much harder to get going than to keep going.

To get past the empty screen, try writing your introduction twice. The first time, just try to get something down on paper. Don't worry about how it sounds or if it works as the perfect introduction to your paper. It probably doesn't. After you finish your paper, go back and rewrite your introduction. You'll find that it's much easier to handle because your entire paper is laid out in your mind.

A good introduction catches the reader's interest, clearly states the paper's thesis, and briefly suggests what arguments and analyses you'll use to support your main claim. Although it doesn't have to be, your thesis statement is usually stated in the last sentence of your introduction. Most students prefer to put it last and use it as a launching pad for the rest of the paper.

The introduction is one of the most creative parts of your paper, and there is no formula for writing a good one. Try to be original, but don't be too gimmicky. Don't start with a fictional narrative unless you're really comfortable writing fiction. Begin with a quote if you want, but make sure that it's relevant to your topic and is there for a purpose.

Many of us learned the "funnel" model for the introduction in high school: It starts with a broad claim and moves to a clear and specific thesis statement. There's some validity to this idea. Especially on the first draft of your paper, it can help to start with some general ideas about your topic and move to the focus of your paper—your thesis.

Some students take the idea of a funnel way too seriously. We've heard a few professors joke about the "primordial ooze" introduction in first-year papers: "Since he emerged from the primordial ooze, man has always wondered about (insert topic here) . . ." This kind of introduction doesn't get you very far. Whatever general statements you write at the beginning of your introduction, make sure that they're related to your topic and that you use them to set up your thesis.

And Therefore . . .

Topic sentences are a great way to organize a paper because they force you to view the work as a whole, with a logical progression from start to finish. Think of the topic sentences as bones in the skeleton of the paper. Don't just start writing paragraphs as they come to you, or you'll end up with quite a disfigured body.

—Sophomore
Northwestern University

Disclaimer: If you think for a moment that you hear your high school English teacher talking, you're not entirely wrong. Most likely, all of our English teachers harped about transitions between sections and paragraphs. It turns out that they did it for a reason—a lack of good transitions in your paper can confuse your professor and cause him or her to not understand or misinterpret the logic and flow of your arguments.

Transitions are important because they explain to your reader how each part of your paper is connected to the others, and they give him or her a sense of direction for what's to come. Good transitions will make your paper read much easier and your professor will be able to actually think about what you're saying rather than try to get oriented in your paper.

Begin each paragraph with a transition that links it to the one preceding it. You may have learned lists of transition words in high school (words like "however," "therefore," and "furthermore"). Make friends with these words as you write, but make sure that your transitions don't sound too similar or repetitive.

Here's one example of a good first transition sentence in a paragraph:

> The lack of equality between the lovers apparent in Browning's poem "Porphyria's Lover" contrasts with the relative equality we find between the loved and the beloved in his "Two in the Campagna."

The first part of the sentence likely links the new paragraph to the one before it. The sentence also gives us some sense of what this paragraph will be about. It looks like the writer has just discussed the relationship of the lovers in "Porphyria's Lover" and will begin to analyze the relationship in "Two in the Campagna." As readers, we know where we've been and where we're going.

Your first sentences don't need to be this formal. But they should connect each paragraph to the one before it and capture, at least in part, the main point that you're about to discuss.

Quote Like a Pro

Quotes are like the evidence a lawyer presents to a judge. They are the only concrete things you have. You should use them to support your arguments.

—Sophomore
Cornell University

Many papers you write in college will require you to include quotes from one or more sources. Even if you don't have to do it, integrating a few quotes into your writing can add life and persuasiveness to your arguments. The key is to use quotes to support a point you're trying to make rather than just include them to fill space.

There are a few simple ways to use quotes in your paper. The first is not to quote at all and instead summarize the main points of a source. This approach works well for sources where the particular language of the quote is not especially important. If you're writing about history, paraphrasing is sometimes a great way to use secondary materials (the work of other historians and scholars) in your paper.

Another way to use source material is to quote a key word, phrase, or sentence that captures the essence of the text you're writing about. For example, if your paper is an attempt to explain the popularity of a Republican president, and you're quoting a book by a very liberal writer, you might use the phrases "dynastic succession" and "crack monkey" in your paper. Carefully chosen words and phrases can really bring out your own arguments.

A third way to use quotes is to quote directly a whole block of text. These are called block quotes and are usually single-spaced, placed in smaller font, and indented from the margins of the page. These are useful if there is a very rich passage in a source that is essential to your argument.

Make sure to connect quotes to your own arguments and to use them to make your own points stronger. Analyze each quote you include, explain why it's significant and how it affects your own point. Professors hate seeing a bunch of quotes in a paper without understanding why they're there or what you intend to do with them beyond filling some space. Don't fall into this trap.

You should also make sure that the phrases and sentences you quote from other sources fit grammatically into your prose. For example:

> The Backstreet Boys were an oasis in the cultural desert that was the late 1990s. Always modest, they never bragged about the impact they had on the development of a whole new genre of boy-band music. In an MTV interview, they said that they merely hoped to "making beautiful songs."

See the problem? The writer didn't adjust the quote to fit grammatically into the last sentence. The quote should have been adjusted to read:

> They merely hoped to "mak[e] beautiful songs."

Use brackets to change verb tenses and clarify ambiguous pronouns (an undefined "he" or "she"). You can also adjust your own sentences to better align with the quotes. Whatever you do, make sure that you use quotes in a way that works grammatically with the rest of the sentence.

Stealing Is Wrong

Plagiarism is passing off someone else's words or ideas as your own. You've probably heard about it since kindergarten, and you'll hear about it forever because it never goes away. People, including college students, continue to plagiarize—from books, articles, and from each other—and although some get caught, many more get away with it. But what fun is knowing that the A you got on your paper was not for you, but for the author of the paper you found on the Internet?

We won't preach about the moral issues of plagiarism, although there are many. And we won't remind you more than once that your own conscience will probably eat away at you if you blatantly plagiarize. Sticking to our mission of providing you with only the most practical and relevant information, we'll mention a few practical reasons not to plagiarize.

You can get caught, most definitely. TAs and professors have spent years reading through books, articles, and other papers related to your class, and chances are, they'll recognize when you're plagiarizing. They'll also be able to sense if the level and style of your usual writing suddenly changes when you hand in your paper. Then you're in trouble—ranging from a low grade to getting kicked out of school, depending on how much you plagiarize and how strict your school is. Don't do it.

On the flip side, you want to avoid being wrongly accused of plagiarism by carefully citing all of your sources. Find out what kind of citation system your professor prefers and use it. You don't need to put in citations for general knowledge: Uncontested dates, the authors of major works of literature, and basic historical facts don't need citations, for example. Anything else that's not your own work needs a citation. If you're not sure, cite the source anyway. It's better to have a few unnecessary footnotes than be accused of plagiarism.

One final reason not to plagiarize: You don't need to do it. You're smart enough and able enough to have great thoughts on your own. Why would you need to steal someone else's?

Papers For Sale

Yup, you can get a college paper from the Internet. Numerous paper depositories have sprung up in the last few years offering you A+ papers on any topic and for any class. All you have to do is fork over a few bucks and you're done with your paper assignment. Easy, right?

Not really. First of all, how do you know that the papers offered by these services are any good? You don't know and you have no way of finding out. Why would you trust someone else to write a better paper than you could if you have no idea about who the author is?

More important, however, if you bought a paper from one of these Internet services and turned it in as your own, you'd be plagiarizing big time.

Some students say that they check out Internet paper services to get ideas about how other people have approached similar topics. This doesn't sound so bad. But the temptation to plagiarize from the paper you're reading can be too great if you like what you see—it's right in front of you, you have two days to write your paper, you have another final in a day, and it would be so easy just to copy whole sections from someone else's paper.

Have some faith in yourself and leave Internet papers to someone else. You're smart enough to write your own.

Style Guide

You'll do fine on your paper if you have a strong thesis and your supporting arguments and points are well organized and clearly expressed. But to really ace it you should try to make your writing style distinctive in some way.

Learning to write with style is nothing any of us can learn to do overnight, but developing a distinctive personal style in your papers is not a bad goal to have as you write more of them. Reading great books and well-written magazine articles can help you improve your own writing style if it's something you're thinking about as you read.

Learning to write with flair—in a way that presents your ideas clearly but not in a dull academic tone—is worth a shot. You'd be surprised how far it can get you.

All Good Things Must Come to an End

In high school, you may have learned that the conclusion is a summary of your thesis followed by a brief explanation of the broader relevance of your arguments.

This basic structure is useful, so keep it in mind. You should try to encapsulate the overall thrust of your main argument or analysis in your conclusion. Don't give a long-winded summary of every major point you discussed in your paper, but try to remind your reader of your thesis and its key supporting arguments.

It can sometimes be useful to think of what your thesis implies about a particular work of literature, a particular time period, or a particular person that you wrote about. But if you write about the "broader relevance" of your topic, try not to get too carried away. Stick to your topic. Human nature, the cosmos, reality, and the nature of history are all favorite topics for some of the most uninteresting and trite conclusions.

Even if it sounds great at three in the morning on the day you're handing in your paper, don't write something like: "The debate on this topic will continue for the rest of human history." It doesn't say very much.

Have some fun with your conclusion and try to be a bit creative. It's a good place to use some appropriate humor or make a subtle point that's outside the scope of your paper. There's no need to be overly profound or clever, and if you can make your professor smile or pause to think for a moment, you'll leave a good last impression.

In your conclusion, try to avoid repeating what you've already said. And ask yourself, so what? Why would anyone want to read this paper?

—Junior
Carleton College

Work Hard, Play Hard

Try to take a few breaks as you write. Our brains get tired, and when they're tired they tend not to be as sharp. Have you ever read what you wrote after hours of writing and not know what in the world you meant by it?

Give yourself some room to breathe. Get away from your paper—even if it's just for a few minutes—and you'll have more mental energy when you begin to work on it again.

We Talk With . . .

Rachel,
Sophomore, Franklin and Marshall College

What has been the most difficult paper you wrote in college? Why was it so difficult?
The most difficult paper I wrote was any paper for my philosophy class because that class made me realize that I hated philosophy, and I had a hard time adjusting to a different style of writing. I was also intimidated by a paper for my Renaissance lit class where we had to cite the Oxford English Dictionary and could not have any citation errors, but that paper ended up going really well.

What is most helpful to you in getting your college papers done?
My friend has an MLA handbook that I steal whenever I need to write a paper.

What advice would you give to college students about writing college papers?
I procrastinate because I can never get anything done otherwise. I found that it's best to start my papers (the actual writing, not including research) two or three days ahead of time so I won't have to be up all night the night before it's due. Also, know exactly what your professors want in the paper; if they say one page, do not write three. And "save" frequently!!!!

5

Revisions Time

Even if you only have a few hours before you have to hand in your paper, try to revise it at least once. Print out your first draft, get away from your computer, and read your paper with as much of an independent and critical eye as you can. Make sure that your ideas and arguments make sense, that they're presented in the most effective order, and then comb through your paper looking for spelling and grammar errors. Over and over we hear professors get annoyed at papers that have great content but are poorly edited.

The hard part is over. You've got your first draft on paper and the blank computer screen with an impatient cursor is no more. Put some extra effort into revising and editing your paper and you'll avoid getting a lower grade for something you worked hard to get right.

- Mental Yoga
- Not Your Own Eyes
- Take a Step Back
- Caution: Passive Voice
- Spice It Up
- Don't Be a Brown Nose
- Sweat the Small Stuff

Mental Yoga

One of the least effective ways to revise a paper is to start making corrections and moving around material right after you finish your conclusion. You need a fresh pair of eyes to really get somewhat of an objective perspective on something you've just spent hours staring at. Take a break, even if it means coming back to it tomorrow.

—Sophomore
Northwestern University

Even if it's the night before your paper is due, you should try to take some time to step away from your keyboard. If you try to revise too soon, you won't be a very critical reader. If at all possible, you need to put some space and time between your mind and your paper.

Play Monopoly, go for a walk, watch TV, have a water-balloon fight, eat a cookie. Do anything that isn't related to school or to your paper.

Once you feel more relaxed and refreshed, carefully read and reread your paper. Print it out and write notes on it as you revise.

The Writing Process

by Robert, Junior,
University of Oregon

What has been most helpful to me in writing papers for college is developing some sort of a process. In high school I used to write papers in one big push, which basically consisted of me sitting down the night before the paper was due and just writing, doing research as I went. Back then, my goal was simply to write the best paper I could in the shortest time possible. While this worked quite well at the time, I've found that as I progressed to higher level classes and gotten deeper into subject matter, this approach to writing was not only ineffective, but very stressful as well.

These days, I leave plenty of time to research the subject of the paper as much as necessary, and make sure I have a thorough understanding of what the paper is about. I find that looking into what I'm going to write about is well worth the time, because it makes the entire writing process much smoother. It allows me to gain a better sense of the material, not only objectively, but what my own opinions are as well.

After researching, I like to write a brief outline, or at least think a little about what I am trying to prove, and what my main points and arguments are. Then I'll usually just sit down and write as much as I can, and worry about editing and revising later. For a paper of seven pages, I'll usually spend a day researching and developing ideas, two days writing, and one day revising and editing. That's how I do it, but it's important for each person to develop a process they feel comfortable with, and in a time frame that allows their writing to come naturally.

Looking at something on the screen is not the same as holding it in your hand.

As your read, try to be methodical. Read your paper at least twice: once to get a sense of the overall content and flow and a second time to look for spelling and grammar problems. When you come across something you need to change, don't run to your computer right away. Take time to let it sink in before you start deleting whole paragraphs.

Not Your Own Eyes

You should strongly consider having someone else read a draft of your paper. Because you've spent so much time planning and writing it, you aren't the most critical judge of its flaws. Give it to someone whose opinion you trust, and who will take the time to read it carefully. Ask a friend, or take it to your school's writing center or workshop.

The writing centers at most schools are great resources and the students who work there have a lot of experience looking at student papers. Plus, unlike your roommate, they don't have to sleep ten feet from you for the next eight months. They have no reason to try to be nice rather than critical.

Ask your reader if he or she can follow your thesis, main arguments, and analyses. Do they make sense or is something confusing? Can your reader tell you what your thesis is after reading the introduction? Do your arguments seem well organized?

Listen carefully to the feedback you hear and try not to be too defensive. At the same time, don't necessarily assume that your reader is right and you're wrong. If it's a subjective point—your reader thinks that your thesis is too contentious or that your second argument should go before your first, for example—there can be different ways to approach it. Think about the comments you get on your paper, evaluate them, and stick to your instincts if you really think that you've got the right approach.

Take a Step Back

Look at your thesis and your core arguments. Now is the time to ask yourself if your thesis and your paper make the same point. If they don't, check to see if perhaps you reached a different conclusion by the time you finished your writing. Sometimes we start writing and arguing a certain point, but as we think about it and write more, we end up developing an argument for a slightly different one—or a drastically different one, in some cases. If you see a shift of focus in your paper as you revise, think for a moment whether you might need to alter your original thesis.

It might help to write out your original thesis statement on a separate piece of paper and refer to it as you read through your first draft. That way, you'll always have it in front of you and can easily judge if your paper is going in a different direction.

Caution: Passive Voice

Here's another "this sounds like my high school English teacher" piece of advice: Don't use too much of the passive voice in your paper.

The passive voice is a combination of a form of the verb "to be" (is, was) and a verb.

The active voice eliminates the "to be" verb and places the verb in the past, present, or future tense. Here are a few examples:

PASSIVE: was running/were being chased
Biff **was running** from the giant poodle.
The Backstreet Boys **were being chased** by giant poodles.

ACTIVE: ran/chased
Biff **ran** from the giant poodle.
Giant poodles **chased** the Backstreet Boys.

It's not necessarily wrong to use the passive voice. Sometimes it works and might be the only way to make a point. But in general, stick to its active counterpart. It makes your writing sound powerful and more direct. The active voice is easier to understand and more clearly expresses your point. Many professors say that the passive voice sounds more abstract and tentative, and abstract and tentative is not what you want to sound like in your college papers.

I think people sometimes overcompensate by avoiding the passive voice completely. Focus on varying your sentence structure instead.

—Sophomore
Carleton College

Spice It Up

I used the word "indeed" fifteen times in one of my papers. The paper was four pages long. It was an obsession that I had to kick, but it wasn't easy. Once you like a word it just seems to type itself on the keyboard.

—Junior
Wesleyan University

In the same way that most of us talk in recognizable speech patterns, we tend to fall into patterns in our writing. Some of us write a lot of long, winding sentences. Others tend to write short, choppy sentences. Some of us tend to overuse qualifications like "but" and "however," while others don't use them enough.

Read your paper and make sure that your sentences don't all sound alike.

✓ Do you use the same words again and again?
✓ Do you start every sentence with a preposition?
✓ Do you use the word "however" in the first sentence of every paragraph?
✓ Do you use the word "holistic" on every page?

Scott's Corner

In my papers, I have a tendency to write really long sentences. When I'm revising my writing, I look carefully for places where I write too many of them in a row. If a section seems difficult to understand, I add a short sentence, or rewrite parts of the paragraph to include one or two short sentences. I had an English teacher in high school who told me to "punctuate my prose" with short sentences. That's not a rule that I hold to all the time, but it sometimes helps to make my writing sound more direct and forceful.

Some consistency of style is important because it leads to a distinctive, personal voice. Without making your writing too inconsistent, though, you should try to vary your sentence structure. Mix longer sentences with shorter ones. Look for repetitive words and substitute different ones. Make your writing interesting to read and your professor will breeze through your paper rather than become bored by it.

Don't Be a Brown Nose

Even if your paper is about *Hamlet*, you shouldn't go out of your way to flatter the author. No matter how much you adore Shakespeare, don't start off by saying, "As the greatest genius to ever write in the English language, Shakespeare has tremendous insight into the nature of human grief." Even if most people agree that Shakespeare is unparalleled, it sounds a bit pretentious to write this in your paper.

Some professors dislike these kinds of statements because they can sound like attempts to win brownie points. By kissing up to the author, it can seem like you're kissing up to the professor. You can also create the impression that you're trying to make up for other deficiencies in your paper by saying how much you loved the material on which it's based.

This doesn't mean that all flattery is out of the question. Just make sure not to overdo it, and that when you flatter, it's for some reason that's related to your paper.

Sweat the Small Stuff

Most professors are probably more interested in the quality of your writing and your ideas than technical perfection. As you revise, first spend time polishing the content of your paper before you spend hours working on mechanics.

On the other hand, all professors appreciate writing that's technically correct. Many of the papers they read are full of typos, spelling errors, and bad grammar. If you take the time to carefully proofread your paper, your professor will be impressed and won't be distracted from your ideas and arguments.

Read through your paper once to focus on grammar and spelling. Look for minor errors of all kinds—misplaced commas, uncapitalized names, and incomplete sentences—and make changes. Be sure to double-check the spelling of the author's names and titles of the works that you cite in your paper.

Scott's Corner

I was on campus after finals for a few days during my sophomore year, and I asked one of my professors if I could meet with him to discuss my final paper. I spent probably over forty hours on it, including research, planning, and writing. By the time I turned it in, it had grown to almost thirty pages.

I was very interested to hear my professor's comments, partly because the paper was so long, and partly because it would be my only formal grade in the class for the entire semester. When I walked in to his office, I'm sure that I was visibly nervous. (I look nervous most of the time, so I probably looked absolutely terrified.)

It's easy to swallow a bad grade on a paper in the relative anonymity of a classroom, but it's a little more uncomfortable to read through thirty pages covered in red when your professor stares at you through his tortoise-shell glasses. Despite my best efforts at proofreading, I noticed quickly that I had misspelled the name of the city that I was writing about consistently for at least half the paper. Additionally, I misspelled the name of one of my primary sources every time I used it.

He took my sloppiness as a personal affront. We had developed a good relationship over the previous semester, and he had given me lots of valuable advice as I worked toward a thesis. He had even given me a book at the end of the semester as a way of acknowledging my hard work on this paper. Fortunately, he understood that I was so burned out by the time I finished the paper that I simply didn't see the mistakes in my final draft.

You've heard this before, of course, but here's a friendly reminder: Don't rely on your computer's spell check or grammar check to catch all errors. It will find and fix some glaring errors, but it can't tell where you mean to say "there" vs. "their." Only your own eyes can catch word-usage problems, so read through your paper carefully.

For details on proper grammar and word usage, check out some helpful books we've included in the Helpful Resources chapter of this guide. They can provide much more extensive help than we're qualified to present.

Before you hand in your paper and sigh with relief, quickly check to make sure that your pages are numbered, your name and paper title are on the first page, and that you staple your pages in the correct order.

Phew, now sigh with relief!

We Talk With . . .

Rebekah,
Sophomore, Bryn Mawr College

How do you think college papers differ from papers you had to write in high school?
In addition to being better written (little slack is given for grammatical errors) and better organized, there tends to be a heavier emphasis on research in college. At Bryn Mawr, we are frequently instructed to choose topics for our final papers up to a month in advance, to accommodate ordering special or hard-to-find materials from other libraries around the country. You cannot get by with

simply "Googling" your topic or drawing from only one or two general sources.

What is most helpful to you in getting your college papers done?

Submitting early drafts to your professor, or meeting with them to bounce ideas back and forth, is incredibly helpful for making sure you're on the right track as you write the paper. The professor may remind you of some facet of your topic or important argument you may have overlooked. Meeting with a professor is also very useful at the very beginning of the paper-writing process, when you're still defining your topic.

What advice would you give to college students about writing college papers?

Don't let the small stuff—like proofreading—get put off to the very last minute. I remember once staying up till 4:00 am writing a paper that was due at 10:00 that morning. I figured I'd crash and then have a friend look it over for typos and minor grammatical errors the next morning. (Another pair of eyes can prove very useful for proofreading—recruit your roommate whenever you can!) I figured this process would only take a few minutes, but a friend and I were still frantically correcting the draft and reprinting pages until ten minutes after my class had started! I entered my class breathless and red-faced, clutching the freshly printed paper in my hand. Thankfully, my professor still accepted it, although he did shoot me a disapproving frown.

6

Research-Project Strategies

Some college papers require that you conduct independent research outside of class materials. These papers can be a bit more difficult to write because they require you to say something original about something you have to learn on your own. In general, though, a research paper is quite similar to any other paper in that it has a central thesis you have to support with evidence you find in your research. If you can tackle a regular college paper, you can tackle a research one.

The following sections offer some specific tips and advice about approaching a research paper.

- Can You Handle It?
- Roll with the Punches
- You've Got to Have Purpose

- Read the Boring Stuff
- Recordkeeping
- You Can't Be Too Creative
- Have a Battle Plan for Each Source
- Plan It Out
- No Plan Is Set in Stone

Can You Handle It?

When choosing a topic for your research paper, keep in mind that you'll need to have access to enough materials to complete your research in a limited amount of time. Choosing an amazingly interesting topic will do you no good if you can't find enough sources to do thorough research.

To know whether you can tackle your topic with enough resources, do some preliminary research before you really settle on it. Run a few searches on your library's computer catalog. See how many books on your topic you can find, and read a few chapters out of them.

Keep in mind that you can get access to a tremendous number of resources by using the Internet. Many newspaper and magazine articles are now available online and a few Internet libraries allow you to access whole books on your screen (www.questia.com is one example).

You want to make sure that you can adequately research your topic without going crazy looking for sources and having to make arguments without enough supporting evidence. Put in

some effort before settling on your final topic and you'll probably save yourself a great deal of frustration later on.

Roll with the Punches

If you're writing a research paper on a somewhat unfamiliar topic,
you might discover ideas in your research that you hadn't initially
anticipated. Unlike papers based on materials you've already read,
you won't know what you're getting yourself into when you start
your research. Keep an open mind and be willing to change the direction of your paper as you dive deeper into your research.

In fact, you should expect your topic and your thesis to evolve
as you read. That's the point of research—to learn about a particular topic in detail and figure out exactly what you want to say
about it.

You've Got to Have Purpose

Researching can actually be really fun and you might find yourself completely engrossed in reading about the art of the Javanese
Gamelan. (No, really.) It can be easy to lose your sense of direction and purpose in your research and to end up having re-
searched some pretty interesting but irrelevant information for
your paper. If you had all the time in the world, that would be
just fine, but you're in college and you're busy, so you need to research for a purpose.

The purpose of your research is to find evidence to support the main arguments of your paper and your thesis.

Before you dive head first into your research, take a moment and think about your topic. Chances are, you know something about it already. Can your formulate a preliminary thesis? You might want to read through the first few sources you've gathered and then jot down some ideas. Your thesis doesn't have to be extremely specific at this point, but it will help to actually have a direction as you begin to research and look for more sources.

At the same time, make sure that you're flexible as you research and don't stay too wedded to your initial thesis. Remember that it was just an initial idea to give you direction and it can change significantly as you research and find evidence that either supports your initial position or argues against it. Try to keep as much of an objective mindset as you can when you research, and be open to learning things that you hadn't anticipated.

Read the Boring Stuff

When you start compiling sources for your paper, you should make an effort to read the footnotes and bibliographies of the sources that you find most useful. Nobody likes reading bibliographies, but if you do, you'll get a much better idea of other sources you should consider. You'll save yourself a lot of time trying to find related sources using your library's card catalogue or searching on the Internet.

Recordkeeping

It's really important to keep good notes as you research. Your mind might be brilliant and remember everything now, but things have a tendency to fade with time. You can save yourself a lot of anxiety and frustration later on if you write down the important ideas and specific points as you discover them.

Make sure to write down the most significant points that you find in each source, the corresponding page numbers, and the exact name of the source. Use Post-It notes to mark important passages in books and articles.

If you keep good records, you'll be able to organize your notes easily as you make your outline. You'll also avoid plagiarizing by having a clear record of where your ideas came from. It can be very easy to absorb ideas from one source and think they're your own.

Scott's Corner

Last year, I had to write my first big research paper, a thirty-page beast of an assignment. I'd never used notes for a research paper before, and I didn't think that I would ever need to. At first this worked out fine, but as I got to my twentieth book about commerce in South India in the sixteenth century, my mind was a blur. Somehow, I managed to pull together something halfway decent for my final paper, but it took much longer than it should have. I spent more time sifting through books than I did writing my paper. I would spend fifteen minutes looking for one passage that I needed and another ten minutes rereading what I'd already read.

You Can't Be Too Creative

Be really creative about finding useful and unique sources for your paper. See if you can find organizations related to your topic and scour their discussions, reading lists, reports, and other data. Many conferences now post their discussions and presentations online as well. Find those that are relevant and get a hold of the materials.

Remember also that the sources you'll be using won't always be in print form. There may have been a great documentary film on the topic, a radio show, or a symposium. Check out these sources—you can find some unique information to really improve the quality of your paper and your professor will be impressed.

Also remember that your professor is a great resource for helping you with your research. He or she has probably read a lot of material on your topic and can suggest where you should look.

 Primary Colors

Primary sources are those created and left behind by the participants of historical events, such as letters, diaries, manuscripts, and newspaper articles written at the time of these events. Primary sources allow you, the researcher, to get as close to these historical events as possible, and to formulate your own conclusions about them.

As you research, you should aim to locate as many primary sources related to your topic as possible.

Secondary sources are interpretations of primary sources created after certain events took place. A history textbook is a great example of a secondary source. Milk secondary sources for what they're worth—great syntheses of information, summaries of analyses, and opinions on particular topics.

Have a Battle Plan for Each Source

Chances are, you're not going to have enough time, patience, or interest to read through each of your sources in detail. And there's really no need to do this. What you do need to do is find information in your research that reveals something about your topic and your thesis.

With this in mind, there will be many sources from which you read just a few pages, or even just a paragraph. To make sure that you can find the critical information without wasting time, develop a system for how you'll work with each source. Here are a few suggestions:

✓ Check the book's table of contents to find the most relevant sections.

✓ Skim through the introduction. This is usually the road map to the book or article, and it will help you focus on the source's key sections.

✓ After you find relevant chapters or sections, read them and take notes. Write down enough information so that it will make sense to you when you read it later, but avoid taking down sentences word for word.

✓ Check out the footnotes in the relevant sections and the bibliography as discussed earlier.

You can use these steps as your guidelines and add your own, but just remember to have a plan of attack for each source rather than spending your valuable time browsing through pages after pages without a clear direction.

Plan It Out

Even more than for other papers, an outline is a vital tool for writing good research papers. It's a way to summarize and consolidate your research into clear and logical arguments.

As we've already mentioned, don't use your outline to write down every point that you'll address in your paper. Use it to plan the structure of your paper and the general shape and flow of your arguments.

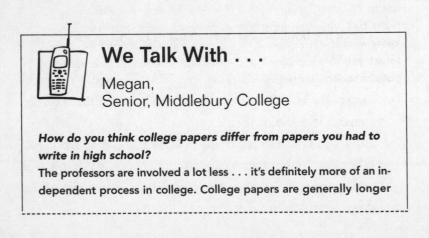

We Talk With . . .

Megan,
Senior, Middlebury College

How do you think college papers differ from papers you had to write in high school?
The professors are involved a lot less . . . it's definitely more of an independent process in college. College papers are generally longer

and there's usually a lot more riding on them, in terms of what percentage of your grade they represent. Professors also expect you to be able to adapt to different formats—it isn't just the same structure for each paper. You have to pay attention to what the teacher wants and expects and yet at the same time be original. College professors don't fall for using big words.

What is most helpful to you in getting your college papers done?

I have to work in the computer lab or the library. I can't do it otherwise, I just get way too distracted. And outlines help, too, but if you're doing an outline just to put off actually writing the paper, stop, and just do it. You can always edit it later, and sometimes it's better just to let the ideas flow.

What advice would you give to college students about writing college papers?

Ideally, you should leave a lot of time to work on a paper. But that actually doesn't work for me. I need the pressure of deadlines . . . so I guess it's really up to the person. Just leave yourself enough time and *do not* get into the habit of asking for extensions and handing stuff in late. Once you get in that habit, it's hard to get out of it. I saw a friend fall into that trap and the situation got really bad. Also, be willing to experiment some. Make sure you know what the teacher wants, but be original and don't be afraid to use your own structure and ideas, not just quotes and reiterations of something you read.

No Plan Is Set in Stone

As you write your paper, don't forget to refer to your sources. Often. If you write just from your outline, your notes, and your memory, you risk missing important points and nuances. Your outline should remind you of where you are in your paper and where you're headed, but you should try not to substitute it entirely for your sources.

Surround yourself with the books that you used to generate your outline, and reference them as you write. Your paper will be richer and you'll be able to find great quotes or passages to give life to your arguments.

Conquering Your Senior Thesis

7

An undergraduate thesis is a research and position paper that many of us choose to write during our senior year of college. You can think of it as a really long research paper that takes one or two semesters and lots of brain cells to complete. It's definitely the cause of much stress and anxiety, but also of pride we feel holding the heavy bound copy of our intellectual labors once it's finished. For many of us, our thesis is the longest piece of writing we will ever produce.

Everything you love and hate about working on a research paper is exacerbated tenfold in a thesis. It's longer, it requires much more reflection and intricate planning, an ability to sift through ridiculous amounts of information, and perhaps most of all, it requires that you continue to push yourself for what seems like a never-ending period of time.

- Topic Choices
- Advise Me, Oh Wise One
- Advisor Advice
- The Writing Oddysey

However brilliant of a writer you may be, writing a killer thesis will be a challenge. A thesis requires that you not only research a particular topic in detail, but that you choose and argue a position on it, and do this through clear and cohesive writing.

In addition to the tips on writing for college that we've put together in this book, here are a few things to keep in mind when approaching a senior thesis.

Topic Choices

Be Interested in What You Write

For many months, your thesis will occupy a disproportionately large amount of your thoughts. You'll be much happier if you're constantly thinking about something that is interesting and intriguing to you. Being interested in your topic will also improve the quality of your work. The last thing you need is to be bored by your thesis.

This is a somewhat intuitive point, but really do consider it seriously. It's not difficult to be influenced by a professor or someone else and choose a topic that interests them. But that professor is not the one who is going to be writing dozens of pages on this topic and thinking about it day and night. You are. Figure out what genuinely interests you and don't shy away because of someone else's reaction. Suggestions from trusted professors, parents, and friends are great to think about, and you shouldn't brush them aside. But you know best what intrigues you, and you should try to write your thesis about something that does.

> I didn't realize how easy it would be to get bored with my subject matter. When I started, I was thrilled. I thought I'd chosen a topic near and dear to my heart. But, after a few late nights and some bad data, the whole process just wasn't fun anymore.
>
> —Senior
> Harvard University

Have Some Background

A senior thesis is an advanced project. It leaves little room for basic research and discovery on a topic about which you know absolutely nothing. One or two semesters may seem like a long period of time, but it's not enough time to learn about something on both a basic and a very detailed level, and then write a long paper intelligently formulating and arguing a strong thesis.

While you should have some general understanding of your topic, you don't need to have specific and detailed knowledge about it. The main purpose behind writing a thesis is to research a general topic, find a specific area within it on which you want to focus, and then formulate and argue a thesis about that area.

Here's an example. Not knowing anything about Latin American economies is a general issue. Not knowing the details behind Argentina's debt default is a specific issue that might actually make a great thesis topic for someone who has some background in economics and Latin America.

Don't Be an Expert

Having several months to learn about something in extreme detail is a precious opportunity you'll rarely have after college. It would be a shame if you gave it up by writing your thesis on a topic in which you're an expert. True, the end product may be stellar, but you'll miss out on a chance to learn something new, and to learn it well.

> Probably the most rewarding part of working on my thesis was the chance to become an expert on a particular topic.
>
> —Junior
> Wesleyan University

Get Off the Written Path

If the library shelves are filled with books covering the potential subject of your thesis through ten different angles, maybe you should reconsider. Not that you couldn't come up with a brilliant thesis that presents the topic through an eleventh angle (hey, we know you can). But your chances of finding and presenting a strong and innovative argument are greater if you choose something about which hundreds of other academics have not written.

> Frankly, at least in history, the greatest challenge is being able to say something original about your topic, to not just do a book

report on the literature in your research. You need to find a niche for yourself in a preexisting field and aim to write something that contributes to that field.

—Junior
Wesleyan University

Once you have a few ideas for a topic, go to the library and check out a few sources for each. Read through their introductions and a few paragraphs—this will give you an idea of how much has been written on your particular topic and whether you want to choose a different one.

Think About Scope

Whatever topic you choose to write about, make sure that its scope allows you to research and write a well-argued and complete paper. No, it does not have to be a book or a Master's dissertation, but your thesis should be compelling, and to be compelling, it has to be thorough.

Think about the scope of your topic and whether you can adequately explore and write about it in one or two semesters. Arguing a particular view on the history of the world might not be your best bet for a thesis.

Don't Choose in Isolation

You are the final judge of what you want and can write about in your thesis. But it's a good idea to talk about your ideas with a professor or two before you commit. The professor does not have to be your advisor, but he or she should be someone who has knowledge of the subject area you're considering and whose opinion you trust. Professors have seen hundreds of students succeed and fail at writing theses, and they will definitely have some ideas for you.

We Talk With . . .
Kimberly,
Recent Grad, Fairleigh Dickinson University

What has been the most difficult paper you wrote in college? Why was it so difficult?
My senior thesis was the most difficult paper I wrote in college because it was fifty pages that chronicled a changing organization and its effectiveness. It's a difficult task to determine the effectiveness of an organization when there will always be two sides to whether the organization is effective.

What is most helpful to you in getting your college papers done?
Research. Research. Research.

What advice would you give to college students about writing college papers?
Tackle the assignment once it's first assigned to allow yourself time enough to present a quality assignment. Preparation is key, and you will feel more comfortable knowing your paper is up to standard at the completion of the paper.

Contacting professors, graduate students, and even other under-grads before you start is a great way to get some ideas about your topic. People can often be better resources than books when you begin thinking about your topic because they challenge you to express your own ideas clearly.

—Sophomore
Princeton University

Advise Me, Oh Wise One

Finding the right advisor to guide you along your thesis path is really important. It's perhaps more important than many of us initially realize, and too many aspiring thesis writers have suffered because they made their choice without thinking too much about it.

A good advisor will read your work, make comments and suggestions, alert you to sources that you might not have considered, and share his/her insights with you. A great advisor will become your thought partner, working through your arguments, challenging your assumptions, and opening up new ways to consider common issues. He or she will become personally invested both in your work and in its success.

Look for Experience and Expertise

Your advisor will be of little help to you unless he or she is familiar with the general topic of your thesis and is expert in the academic discipline from which it stems. If you're thinking of writing about French intellectual history, your advisor might be from the history or philosophy department, and should have some familiarity with French intellectuals.

Although you probably know the professors in your academic discipline quite well, do some checking. What have they written? What courses have they taught? You should get some pretty strong clues as to whether your topic and your advisor are a good fit.

Find an Advisor Wanting to Advise

Advising a thesis is not as demanding as writing one, but it does add to a professor's workload and responsibility. Your advisor should understand this and should want to do it. It's a good idea to have a casual conversation with your potential advisor about his or her schedule for the year, availability, and ability to devote time to working with you.

Don't take it personally if a professor refuses to be your advisor. Many are too busy, and some say no because they don't feel that they can contribute to your particular topic. You're better off knowing this before you start.

In the best-case scenario, your advisor should also be interested in what you're writing about. Interest invokes thought, and thought and inquisitive questions are something you very much want your advisor to have about your thesis. When you speak to a professor about your thesis ideas, pay attention to his or her level of interest and factor this into your decision.

Personality Counts

Make sure that you work well with your advisor and that your working styles mesh well together. If you're someone who needs an occasional push or deadline enforcement, then your advisor should be someone who is willing to push. If you need encouragement, then your advisor should be someone open to providing it.

The bottom line is that you should feel comfortable working and talking with your advisor. He or she shouldn't make you feel nervous or intimidated or discouraged. You aren't likely to gain much from your advisor's words of wisdom if you cringe at the mere sound of his or her voice.

Advisor Advice

Set Expectations Upfront

Communication is a good thing. Use it. Talk to your advisor early on about how the two of you will work together. Will you have weekly status meetings to discuss where you are and where you might need to be headed in your writing or research? We definitely suggest that you do in fact establish a meeting schedule. But the most important thing is that you and your advisor both know and expect the same—a regularly scheduled meeting if you agreed to it, or a meeting by appointment, if that's what you decided.

Talk about how involved you'd like your advisor to be in your research and your work. Will he or she be reading drafts often? Or are you going to agree on a few times during the year when you'll give your advisor certain chapters on which to comment?

Make sure you know what your advisor prefers in terms of communication between your meetings. Is phone or email better? When is the best time to call? What are your advisor's busiest days when it might not be a good idea to show up at his or her door?

While not everything you might talk about at the beginning will stay consistent throughout, it will get the two of you started on great terms. By showing your advisor that the way you two communicate and the way you receive his or her feedback is important to you, you're showing that you're respectful of his or her time. And, busy professors like to be respected.

Be Proactive

If you want your advisor to recommend a source, ask. If you'd like him or her to read a draft of one of your chapters, ask. If you had a meeting planned and your advisor didn't show up, ask why not.

Be proactive and straightforward. Your advisor is not doing you a favor by being your advisor. He or she has agreed to do it and, as a result, has assumed certain responsibilities. This doesn't mean, however, that your advisor will be proactive with following through on these responsibilities.

That's your job, so don't be shy.

Be Honest

Be honest with your advisor about everything. They are there to give advice, to coach you, support you, as well as grade you.

If you aren't honest with them about the troubles you are having—with procrastination, writing, or anything—how are they supposed to help you? Meet with them often, it will help you stay motivated and focused. Advisors are an excellent resource—for books, inspiration, contacts, and editing. Use them.

—Senior
Hampshire College

There is a chance that your advisor is not someone you'll know well before you two start working together. You may not know his or her quirks and ways of communication very well. And there may come a day when you ask for your advisor's feedback on your work and you can't tell what he or she really thinks. Be honest in admitting this and ask for clarification.

Nataly's Corner

My advisor was a perfectly nice man and we got along wonderfully. But any time I'd ask him what he thought about my thesis, he'd say something so cryptic and ambiguous that I never knew what he really thought of it. "It's judicious," he wrote on one of my mid-semester evaluations.

I never pressed him for a better answer and spent the year in ambiguity stress. "He's British," I'd console myself, "he can't express praise as unabashedly as we Americans do."

Maybe so, but I wish I'd given him a chance to try by pressing him to really tell me what he thought during the seven months before he gave my thesis a stellar final evaluation.

Being honest with your advisor will improve the quality of your thesis and will gain you respect. As students, we don't generally like feeling ambiguous about our academic performance. Don't create unnecessary stress for yourself during this already stressful time.

Prepare for Meetings

Make sure to prepare carefully before going to meet your advisor to make sure you use the time efficiently.

—Senior

Harvard University

It's great if you have a rapport with your advisor and can talk without end during meetings. But chatting for an hour about last night's game or sharing department gossip is not going to help your thesis. For your advisor to help you with, and contribute to, your thesis, your meetings need to be constructive. And—you guessed it—it's your responsibility to make them that way.

Think about the few key questions or issues that you need to discuss prior to the meeting, and tell your advisor upfront what they are. If you have questions about a certain source, bring the source with you. If you'd like your advisor to read a short piece of your thesis, make sure to bring an extra copy. You get the point.

The Writing Oddysey

However great a writer you might be, writing your thesis will be a challenge. There aren't many students who aren't at least somewhat intimidated by the task, and those who claim that they aren't are definitely covering up. Take a deep breath and try to think about how much you're learning. If that fails to encourage you, imagine that in several months this will all be behind you and you'll be thesis-free forever. This one usually works.

Begin to Write Early

I wrote my thesis over spring break. Don't do that.

—Senior
University of Chicago

It's good to have a lot of sources, but you need to know when to stop researching and start writing. If you think you are procrastinating the writing and doing way too much research, you probably need to start writing. Sources are good, but so is your own voice, don't forget to use it and respect it.

—Senior
Hampshire College

Whatever you do, don't wait until you've finished all of your research to begin writing. Don't even wait until you have finished a big chunk of it. Our brains can't hold an unlimited amount of information, and you'll begin to forget important points and details from your first source by the time you read your twentieth. And even if you take notes while you read, looking at your notes two months after you wrote them isn't likely to fully refresh your mind.

Begin to write early, after you've read a few sources and formulated your initial thesis statement. Don't worry at that point about style, organization, or details. Just get some words and sentences and paragraphs on paper and you'll be amazed at how much easier the writing process will become. Writing down your ideas and arguments will clarify them and expose areas you might need to research further. You'll be able to see if your argument flows together or if you're forcing it along. (At which point you'll need to think it through and figure out if you're headed in the right direction and if you need further evidence to support your points.)

Most important, getting words on paper will help you feel less intimidated by the prospect of writing dozens or hundreds of pages. The blinking cursor at the top of an empty computer screen never made anyone feel good or confident. By beginning to write early, you will avoid this ghastly image, and you'll feel more in control of the vast body of research material you've amassed.

As you begin to write, be cognizant of the fact that you're writing in semi-darkness. You haven't yet figured out all of the arguments, ideas, facts, and details that will eventually fill your thesis and your initial paragraphs will probably be very general. As you research more, you'll need to go back to these initial pages and revise them. But you'll already have something to start with, rather than a blank page and a nervous bug in your stomach.

> My biggest challenge was getting started. I locked myself in my room until I got going.
>
> —Senior
> University of Wisconsin

Make Each Chapter Stand on Its Own

> Think about your thesis chapters as a series of related papers. This will make your total page count less daunting as you start, and also keep you organized as you write.
>
> —Senior
> Princeton University

The question of how to structure a thesis and how to break it up into chapters is probably one of the most common. It's unlikely that you've had to write something made up of chapters before your thesis, and although it doesn't seem that difficult, actually finding the right structure for a thesis can be challenging.

How a thesis can be broken up into chapters varies by the type of thesis, the topic, and its academic discipline. Even two theses written on the same exact topic in the same discipline can be structured completely differently by their authors and the authors' preferences. We can't tell you specifically how to structure yours, but we can offer you a few guidelines.

Each chapter should encompass a complete idea or argument. For example, if you're working on an English thesis about a certain writer, perhaps each chapter can discuss a particular period in that writer's life and how it contributed and influenced the writer's works. Or maybe you're writing about two competing theories of economic development in a certain country. You can have a chapter about each of the theories and their backgrounds, and a few chapters that consider important economic events in the country through the two theoretical lenses. You get the point. Each chapter should contain a distinct and complete idea.

Another way to think about this is to imagine taking a chapter of your thesis and making it as a stand-alone paper or article. Does it present an idea and argue it? Does the reader feel like he or she is reading a completed piece of writing rather than a small piece of something larger? You've succeeded halfway in structuring your thesis if each of your chapters presents a clear and complete idea and can stand confidently on its own.

Don't Write a Chapter for Chapter's Sake

The other half of the task of structuring your thesis is making sure that all of the chapters relate to and further the arguments in your thesis statement, and that they're all necessary to make it as strong as possible. You might be able to find a ton of fascinating material on a certain aspect of your topic and write a stellar chapter about it, but that won't make your thesis stronger if this particular aspect of your topic is not relevant to your overall argument. The chapter will be superfluous and will distract the reader. It will weaken your thesis and that's what you don't want to do.

A good mental test is to look at your thesis, taking a chapter at a time. Read your thesis argument and then look through the

Nataly's Corner

I had a bad feeling about my second chapter from the moment I began to write it. It didn't flow or sound right, I hated writing it more than others, and, worst of all, I kept feeling like it didn't belong. Well, it had no business being in my thesis, and I am lucky that my thesis evaluators didn't let their unanimous opinion that it was out of place cloud their entire judgment of my work.

thesis with that particular chapter missing. You should feel like something is missing. You should feel that there is a hole in the argument, that there isn't enough support for one of the assertions your thesis statement makes. Without that particular chapter, your thesis is not as strong as with it. Now you've got the validation for including that chapter in your thesis. Awesome.

As you think about your paper's structure, don't forget to use the short outline we talked about. It presents a quick picture of your thesis and you can use it to test whether there are unnecessary or missing chapters.

Be Willing to Rewrite

You need to write in drafts. The first draft will always be terrible. Be prepared for several drafts to really convey your points.

—Senior
Wesleyan University

You'll be much better off if you begin to write your thesis with the full expectation that much of what you write might eventually end up in the garbage—or in your computer's recycle bin. Tame your ambitions to get it right on the first try and don't stress out when you find that the last ten pages you've just written make absolutely no sense at all. If a good thesis could be written in just one draft, it's unlikely that colleges would allow us to have the whole year or semester to work on it.

Writing a great thesis and working through several drafts of each chapter requires a lot of guts, in addition to persistence and immense patience. Rewriting is different from editing. It is much more structural and fundamental. Only if you have guts will you be able to scrap a paragraph or a section because you think you can present your points better.

If you can find the guts to rewrite what can be made better, your thesis will have the best shot at being stellar. And you'll have the best chance at feeling stellar for having done it, and for not having been lazy and careless. The worst feeling is to be walking back to your dorm after receiving your less-than-great thesis evaluation and feeling your mind get crowded with a bunch of "couldas" and "shouldas."

Think About Your Reader

Yes, someone is actually going to read your thesis. It might be just a few people like your advisor and thesis evaluators. Or, it might be many more if you're ambitious and persistent enough to get parts, or your entire thesis, published later on. But there will be a time when someone else's eyes will glide over the words, sentences, and paragraphs over which you've labored for many months.

Be aware of your reader as you write. Think about the degree of familiarity your intended reader might have with your subject. Figure out what might be worth explaining in more detail and what you can assume your reader already knows.

In general, it's safe to assume that your reader is an educated adult willing and ready to read academic literature. What you shouldn't assume is that your reader is fully versed in the specific terminology and concepts of your particular topic and academic discipline. Sure, it's likely that your future readers will either come from, or be interested in, the academic discipline in which your thesis belongs. But a historian should be able to read and understand your linguistics thesis, and a mathematician should not be confused by your sociology work.

Write clearly, explain esoteric words and concepts, and avoid using overly academic jargon. Each discipline has its jargon, and if you really must use it, then make sure to define your terms.

Don't Overuse Evidence to Impress

Congrats if you've been able to find a ton of evidence to support your thesis and its central argument. That's an accomplishment all its own, so you should be proud. But try to avoid the temptation to include every great fact and figure.

By all means, you should definitely show off your amazing research skills and perseverance. There are many theses that suffer from poorly supported arguments and many thesis writers who don't go to enough lengths to find the necessary research to make their arguments stronger. If you make an argument, you have to support it, and you should do so unabashedly.

What's not a great idea is to include supporting evidence for the sake of showing just how much of it you've found. The reader of your thesis should be persuaded and convinced by your fair and well-supported thesis argument, but not overwhelmed with too many supporting facts.

Impress with your logic, your ability to grasp and present complex issues in a clear and persuasive way, and with your inviting tone and breadth of knowledge. Leave the facts and figures to their proper role of supporting what you say.

Make Your Conclusion More Than a Summary

The core role of the conclusion to your thesis is to summarize the arguments and ideas you've presented, and to reaffirm your thesis statement (although avoid doing this verbatim). But a great conclusion is more than just a summary. In its finest form, it's a diving platform from which the reader can jump off into a much bigger and deeper set of thoughts and ideas that is related to your thesis.

At its base, the diving platform is stiff and firmly connected to the foundation of the pool. That's the beginning of your conclusion, the summary of what you've argued in your thesis, and the key arguments you've presented. But as you go out further onto the diving platform, it becomes more flexible. That's the middle of your conclusion. Here you can connect your thesis and its arguments to some broader issues you'd like the reader to consider. The tip of the diving platform has the greatest range of motion and the power to launch the diver into the air with confident force.

That's the very end of your conclusion, the part where you should feel free to launch your reader's thoughts out of the bounds of your thesis and into the larger sphere of ideas and implications.

A powerful conclusion makes a difference. It's the last thing your reader will read, and we remember what we read first and last with more accuracy than what we read in the middle. Have some fun with it if you have the energy. This is your last hundred meters.

Adults Weigh In

We asked. They answered. Here are a few pieces of advice from professors and writing workshop directors from Dartmouth, Oberlin, Princeton, and Williams. Since your own professors probably share a few of their opinions, it might be good to keep these in mind as you write your papers.

What Is the One Piece of Advice You Would Give to Students About Writing?

First advice: Be able to summarize the paper in a single statement or question, paying attention to the predicate.

Second advice: Read *The Elements of Style*, by Strunk and White, pp. 15–33.

Have an argument to make. A college paper is not (only) a way of proving you did the work, read the book, know the stuff. It's a way of making the material of the course your own by entering into a vital and substantive discussion/debate of it.

Learn the territory. Spend some time getting to know what "makes" an academic paper. And remember that your paper should pass the "So what?" test. Craft an argument worth reading, and craft it with care.

You can't write a really thoughtful paper the night before it's due. I know you think you can; everyone thinks they can. But it's not true. Good writing is inseparable from good thinking, and good thinking takes time. If you have been thinking about your paper for a week, well, then you may be able to sit down and write it the night before.

Where Do You Think Most Students Go Wrong When Writing Their College Papers?

Both before they begin to write and as they're writing, some students don't keep track of the statement they're trying to make or the question they're trying to answer. They should refer to a written version of it at all times.

Students often misjudge the audience's expectations. Many believe that they have to write to please the professor, so they simply repeat all the brilliant things that the prof has already said in class. Or they inflate their prose, using as many abstract nouns as they can. Or they simply don't spend enough time thinking the matter through. And finally, they don't allow themselves time enough to revise.

The problem is what *doesn't* happen before students even begin to write. Some students think that writing a paper is somehow a discrete act, when writing a paper is really just the process by which they communicate all the thinking and knowledge acquisition that has already gone on. Before writing, there has to be reading, and note taking, and talking, and percolating. Then you have a reason to write.

What Can Students Do to Improve Their Writing Over the Long Term?

Write more papers. Edit what you've written.

Revise! A first draft is very often a way of finding out what you want to argue. Once you've gotten there, you need to go back and figure out what is the best strategy for presenting the argument you want to make.

Helpful Resources

Before you turn to writing manuals or other helpful resources, make sure to take advantage of the writing resources your school already offers. Writing workshops, your professors, and TAs are all invaluable—not to mention easily accessible and free—resources, and you should get as much help from them as you need.

What we've tried to do in this section is suggest a few books and websites that you can turn to for help with specific issues like research, grammar, and general language usage.

Books

The Elements of Style, by William Strunk Jr., E.B. White, Charles Osgood, and Roger Angell. Allyn & Bacon, 4th Edition, 2000.

The classic. If you haven't read it yet, you should read it cover to cover. It has more useful ideas about writing in a more accessible format than just about any other book available. It's the kind of book you'll have on your shelf for the rest of your life.

Woe Is I, by Patricia T. O'Connor. G.P. Putnam's Sons, 1996.

This book gives the clearest and most useful summary of English usage that you'll find anywhere. It's very readable, and you might actually laugh as you read about pronouns. It may turn you into a huge grammar geek.

MLA Handbook for Writers of Research Papers, by Joseph Gibaldi. Modern Language Association of America, 5th edition, June 1999.

A very popular—for good reasons—and very useful resource to help you through the researching and writing process. It includes sections on research, narrowing your topic, taking notes, evaluating authors, and formatting your writing, footnotes, and bibliographies. Offers some helpful ways to cite electronic sources. This book is somewhat of a bible in academia. Buy it, use it, keep it on your shelf, and feel like a true academic.

The next few books on our list come from the University of Chicago Press. No, we are not getting paid for including them on our guide. But yes, after scouring the bookstores for useful, intelligent, and non-gimmicky resources, we found that the University of Chicago Press had a kind of monopoly on the market. Here are a few we particularly like:

Manual for Writers of Term Papers, Theses, and Dissertations, by Kate L. Turabian. University of Chicago Press, 6th Edition, 1996.

This is a less technical and overwhelming alternative to the *Manual of Style* and a straightforward and very useful resource. Some of the best sections are Components of a Paper, Bibliographies, and Sample Layouts.

The Chicago Manual of Style: The Essential Guide for Writers, Editors, and Publishers, by John Grossman (Preface). University of Chicago Press, 15th Edition, 2003.

All the possible formats and requirements made it in, and although it's extremely technical, if you use it rather than read it, you'll impress your readers (and graders) with proper academic formatting. Believe us, it counts.

The Craft of Research, by Wayne C. Booth, Gregory G. Colomb, and Joseph M. Williams. University of Chicago Press, 1995.

If you're really serious about doing a great job with your research and not keeling over in the process, use this book. It is filled with suggestions—albeit, written in a very didactic academic style—about structuring your analyses and arguments, using questions and introductions to guide your research, and avoiding common pitfalls. One of the book's greatest qualities is the way it ties research to the overall goal of writing a term paper or a thesis—that is, to present a cohesive, well-researched, and solidly expressed argument.

Websites

www.questia.com Someone felt the pain of thousands of thesis writers searching through library shelves at two in the morning and created Questia, the largest online library where—with an Internet connection and a few dollars per month—you can read through thousands of social science and humanities books, make notes, create footnotes and bibliographies, and never lose track of a single page. Start with a trial membership to check it out.

www.thesaurus.com An easy-to-use online version of the ever-necessary Roget's Thesaurus. You can search for synonyms by word or topic, just like in the book version. So, if you don't feel like flipping pages, this is a great tool.

www.dictionary.com You got it—it's an online dictionary. It's easy to use and always there to help you.

Stress Relievers

Post-It® Flags These little stickers will save your life. Buy a bunch and use them to mark pages and paragraphs. If you're really organized, you can color coordinate by chapter, but no need to get crazy about it.

www.theonion.com This is an absolutely fun and hilarious website that can provide hours upon hours of wonderfully refreshing stress relief. Use it. It will help.

Granola bars They're crunchy. They're filling. They're great frustration absorbers.

The Final Word

No matter how nervous you might be about writing your college papers, try not to write for the grade. Try to write to be convincing and to reveal something about a topic that others have not yet considered. Try to care about what you say. And try to enjoy it. Treat it as an experiment, not an exam.

When you finally hand in a copy of your paper to your professor, you should feel relieved and satisfied. No matter how you do on your paper, it's a great feat just to get it done. You should be pretty proud of yourself.

You'll probably quickly forget what many of your college papers were about, or even what class you wrote them for. But it'll inevitably teach you something about yourself as a writer. And learning about yourself is part of why you came to college in the first place, right?

Good luck, and write on!

Index

tone, 102
in writing, 56–57, 68–69, 95
Supporting Arguments
for thesis, 2, 3, 22, 29–31, 34,
52–53, 73–74, 76, 79, 82, 96,
101, 106
Supporting arguments. *See*
Arguments

Thesaurus
resources for, 111
Thesis. *See also* Senior thesis
clarification of, 22–25, 35, 76
counterarguments for, 35–36
definition of, 1–2, 21
evidence for, 2–3, 22, 29, 34,
52–53, 96, 101
frustration with, 23, 26
in introduction, 50
originality of, 25
revising for, 21–26, 65
student's advice for, 21–26, 65, 105
summarizing for, 105
supporting arguments for, 2, 3, 22,
29–31, 34, 52–53, 73–74, 76,
79, 82, 96, 101–2, 106
transition to, 21, 34
what it's not, 22
Time Management. *See* Deadlines
Tone, 102
Topic Sentences. *See* Sentences, topic;
Writing
Transitions
in college paper, 50–52
in high school, 51
in language, 21, 34, 50–52

Vocabulary
context for, 47–48, 101
for grammar, 53–54
for quotes, 53–54
resources for, 111–12
Voice
active, 66
individual, 95

passive, 66
revisions for, 66–67

Writing. *See also* Arguments;
Revisions
with active voice, 66
for audience, 46–48, 100, 101, 106
citing sources in, 55, 77
in class, 6–7
from class notes, 30
in college, 20, 33, 37, 48, 66, 68,
71
of college paper, 1
communication in, 107
controversy in, 25
counterarguments for, 35–37
deadlines for, 12–13, 18, 38,
43–44, 81
development of, 15, 25
flexibility with, 26, 43, 44
frustration with, 4, 11, 13, 23,
37–38, 49
grammar in, 47–48, 54, 61, 67, 69,
70–71
in high school, 20, 33, 37, 48, 66,
68, 71
improvement of, 3–4, 5, 38, 47
interest in, 19, 20, 113
with intuition, 3, 32, 84
organization of, 33–35, 112
of outline, 31–36, 80
with passive voice, 66
plagiarism of, 20, 54–56
planning for, 12–13, 18, 38, 43–44,
81
for professors, 10–13, 18–19, 49,
81, 105
quoting in, 51–54, 82
reason for, 107
resources for, 105, 109–11
of senior thesis, 83, 85
student's advice for, 11, 20, 24,
26–27, 38, 40, 45, 48, 52,
58–59, 63, 71–72, 80–81, 99,
105–9